DEATH at Papago Park POW Camp

A Tragic Murder and America's Last Mass Execution

JANE EPPINGA

THE History PRESS

Published by The History Press
Charleston, SC
www.historypress.net

First published 2017

Manufactured in the United States

ISBN 9781467135764

Library of Congress Control Number: 2017931815

Notice: The information in this book is true and complete to the best of our knowledge. It is offered without guarantee on the part of the author or The History Press. The author and The History Press disclaim all liability in connection with the use of this book.

CONTENTS

ACKNOWLEDGEMENTS

The work of a book is never entirely the work of one person, and so it is with *Death at Papago Park POW Camp: A Tragic Murder and America's Last Mass Execution*. Now is the time to round up the individuals and organizations that have generously helped me. These include the Arizona Historical Society Library, the National Archives, the Library of Congress, the Judge Advocate Office, the Harry S Truman Library, the Wisconsin Historical Society, the Monroe County (Wisconsin) History Room and the Santa Barbara Historical Society in California. Individuals include the late Bernard Fontana, the late Rhea Robinson and the late Dorothy and Lawrence Jorgensen. Special thanks to Frederic L. Borch III, regimental historian and archivist, the Judge Advocate General's School, U.S. Army, and to Retired Captain Jerry Mason, who shared his magnificent U-boat archive with me. Special thanks to my panel of experts, the Wednesday Lunch Bunch. No book sees the light of day without a publisher and an editor, including Artie Crisp, Hilary Parrish, Anna Burrous and the rest of The History Press staff.

INTRODUCTION

Werner Max Herschel Drechsler received an honorable military burial at Fort Bliss, Texas, on June 17, 1946, a little more than two years after his brutal execution by his German compatriots on March 12, 1944. Drechsler's murder underscores a unique moral dilemma. Was his hanging for treason by his countrymen murder or treason, and did his execution constitute an act of war? Or was it murder? Or was there even a difference? No physical evidence of Camp Papago Park remains today in what is now a residential section in Scottsdale, Arizona, near the Cross-cut Canal. However, during World War II, about 375 Americans guarded more than 4,000 German prisoners at Camp Papago Park and its outlying camps. Once the Germans and Americans were enemies, but after World War II, the dwindling numbers of Americans and Germans held meetings in a spirit of friendship, through a group known as the Camp Papago Trackers, whose creed was "To renew in friendship the association which commenced in anguish."[1]

Former prisoners love to laugh and talk about the great escape attempt through the *faustball* tunnel. They do not care to speak of Camp Papago Park's dark side. Violence by Nazis against anti-Nazi Germans resulted in brutal beatings and death. They deny any knowledge of the Drechsler murder even though they were incarcerated at Camp Papago Park at the time of his execution. However, Americans such as Dorothy and Lawrence Jorgensen served at Camp Papago Park, and they remember well the morning that the Americans discovered Drechsler's corpse hanging from a bathroom rafter. Dorothy took care of the prisoners' records when they

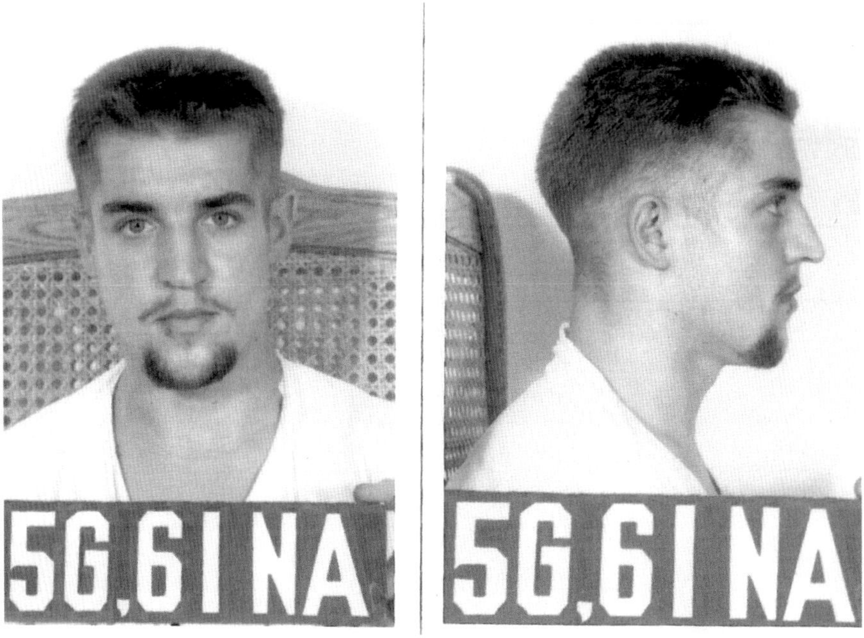

Werner Drechsler, German prisoner of war. *Courtesy National Archives, Washington, D.C.*

arrived and helped them fill out their information cards. Her husband, Lawrence, was a POW guard and became the twenty-sixth man to enter the *faustball* tunnel after its discovery.

The German prisoners asked for permission to create a volleyball or *faustball* court, and the guards provided them with digging tools. Two officers involved with the Werner Drechsler case, Jurgen Wattenberg and Friedrich Guggenberger, were also involved with the great escape through the 178-foot tunnel, which exited near the Cross-cut Canal. Wattenberg ordered the men in the adjacent compound to throw a noisy party the evening of December 23, 1944. At 9:00 p.m., prisoners started crawling out along the tunnel. Next door, their German buddies were singing and breaking bottles. Each escapee carried clothing, food, forged papers, cigarettes and medical supplies. They planned to float down the Cross Cut-canal to the Salt River to the Gila River and on to the Colorado River, which would take them into Mexico. They constructed a raft that could be taken apart. To their disappointment, the Gila River was totally dry.

On December 24, the twenty-five officers and enlisted men had escaped. The escape was discovered when Herbert Fuchs surrendered at the sheriff's

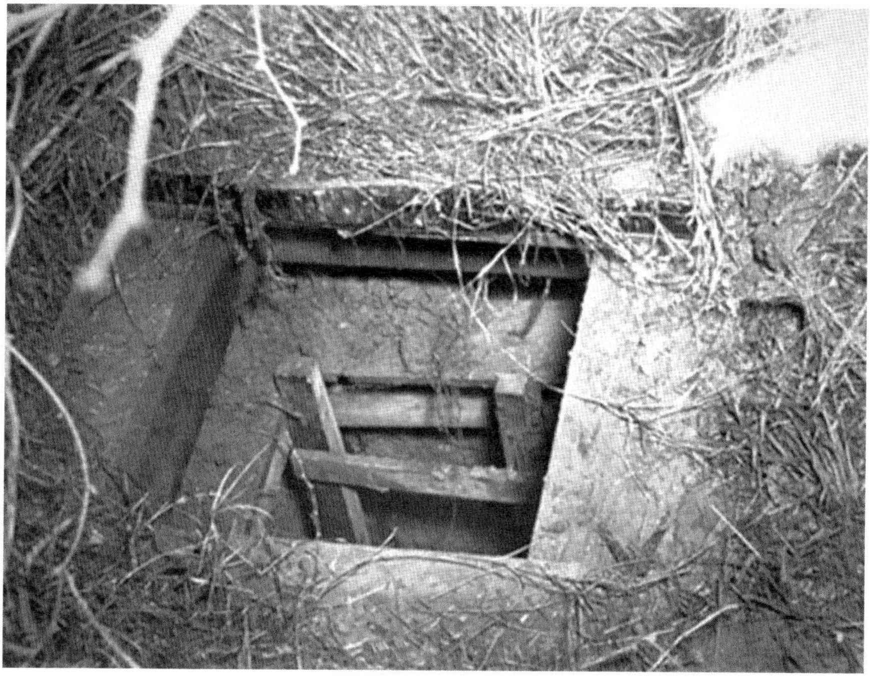

Above: The *faustball* tunnel through which twenty-five German POWs escaped from Camp Papago Park. *Courtesy Dorothy and Lawrence Jorgensen.*

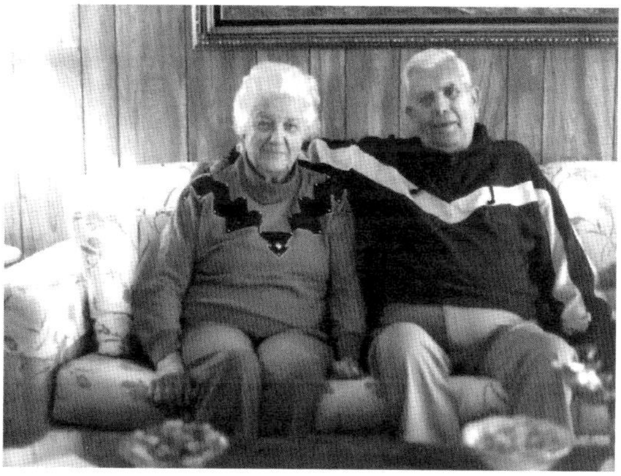

Right: Lawrence Jorgensen served as a guard, and his wife, Dorothy, worked as a secretary at Camp Papago Park. *Courtesy Dorothy and Lawrence Jorgensen.*

office, wet and cold. Several days later, Private Lawrence Jorgensen discovered the camouflaged escape hatch. By the end of the month, Wattenberg had stopped at several Phoenix hotels and asked about a room for the night. He fell asleep in an empty chair in the Hotel Adams lobby. When he left, he was arrested by the police. Near the Mexico border, Guggenberger was arrested and returned to the camp. Jorgensen, who became known as the twenty-sixth man, entered the tunnel and followed it to the end. After a little more than a month, all of the escapees were recaptured.[2]

Arizona became involved in World War II with the surprise attack on the USS *Arizona* at Pearl Harbor.[3] The state's participation in the war effort continued with the raising of the flag by the Pima Indian Ira Hayes at Mount Suribachi; the internment of Japanese Americans in relocation camps; the incarceration of the Japanese consular staff from Hawaii, who gave the orders on where and when to drop the bombs on Pearl Harbor, at a southern Arizona ranch; the large prisoner of war camp established for Italians at Florence in central Arizona; and the numerous German prisoner of war camps throughout the state.

The United States faced the problem of how to treat the flood of enemy prisoners that landed on its shores. After World War I, representatives from forty-seven countries met in Geneva, Switzerland, to discuss the problems of caring for prisoners of war.[4] Signatory nations promised to treat prisoners humanely. Prisoners had a right to clean, safe accommodations and to rations equal in quality and quantity to whatever was served to the detaining power's troops. They were to have access to recreation and to be allowed to buy personal items at military canteens. Representatives from the Red Cross and neutral nations inspected the prison camps.

Prisoners could be kept comfortable in states such as Arizona with a minimum cost of heating fuel. Arizona became a training ground for American soldiers destined to fight in North Africa. Two waves of prisoners of war arrived during World War II. The first group came in 1943 after North Africa's surrender, and the second contingent arrived during the first weeks of the 1944 Normandy landings. At Norfolk, prisoners had medical checks before being sent to various camps.

Submariners at Camp Papago Park were composed of steel workers and mechanics with a rudimentary elementary education plus a few years of trade school. They served under the elite U-boat command of Admiral Karl Doenitz. On April 30, 1945, just before his suicide, Adolf Hitler named Doenitz as his successor. On May 7, Doenitz ordered General Alfred Jodl to sign the German surrender in France.[5]

By the end of 1942, the United States had 1,881 prisoners; a year later, there were 172,879 captives. By 1945, the United States' total POW population had risen to 371,683 Germans, 50,273 Italians and 3,915 Japanese. These numbers did not include incarcerated civilians suspected of operating as enemy aliens. At its peak, Arizona detained more than 6,000 German prisoners of war.[6] Before World War II, Arizona's main source of revenue came from cattle, cotton, copper, citrus and climate.

With the construction of airfields and war-related industries, Arizona's economy shifted to a technology-based financial system.

With the outbreak of World War II, the first order of business was to build internment and concentration camps. Two months after the bombing of Pearl Harbor, President Franklin D. Roosevelt ordered approximately 120,000 Japanese Americans to evacuate the West Coast. They relocated to one of ten internment camps located across the country. The Colorado River Relocation Center had a peak population of 18,000. The Gila River Relocation Center had a population of about 13,000. The federal government was responsible for housing, feeding, employing and providing services for Japanese citizens who had been interned. Engineers designed fenced camps where each block contained fourteen barracks, one mess hall and one recreation hall on the outer edges, with separate laundry and men's and women's lavatories. Households were assigned space in the one-hundred-by twenty-foot family structures of wood and tar paper according to the number of people in the household. Other camp structures were designated

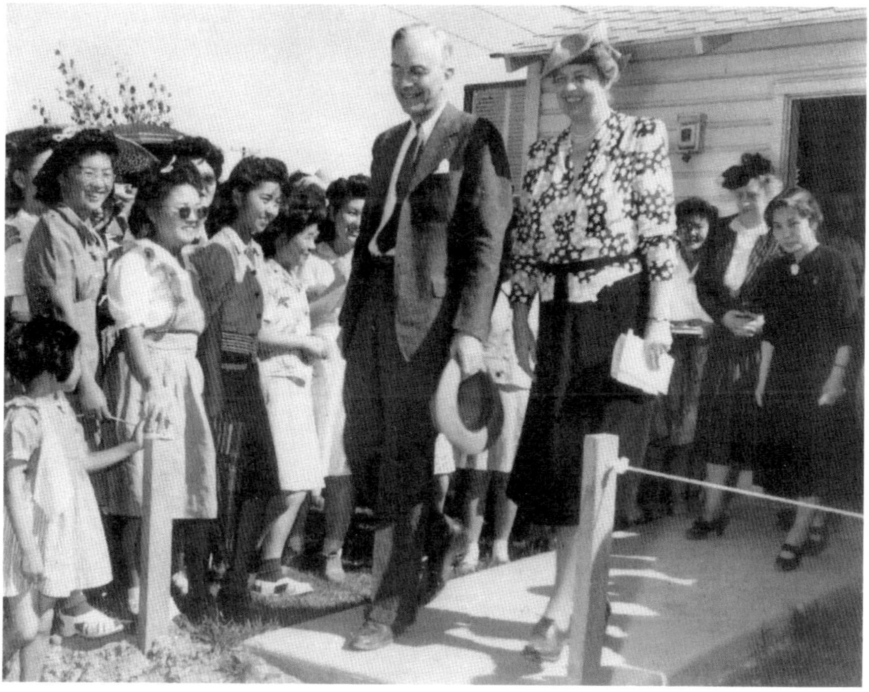

Eleanor Roosevelt and Dillon S. Myer, director of the War Relocation Authority, director of the Federal Public Housing Authority and commissioner of the Bureau of Indian Affairs, visiting the Gila River War Relocation Center at Florence, Arizona, on April 23, 1943. *Courtesy National Archives, Washington, D.C.*

as warehouses, vehicle and equipment repair shops, administration buildings, schools, canteens, library, religious services, hospitals and a post office. Vegetables and fruits were cultivated for camp and commercial consumption, and livestock was bred.[7]

In Florence, located along the Gila River in Pinal County, with a mix of soil, sun and miles of man-made canals, cotton farmers grew the finest long Pima cotton outside of Egypt. Just beyond Florence, the Southern Pacific Railroad spur tracks stop at what used to be the gates of Camp Florence. This POW camp confined sixteen thousand Italian prisoners and a few German prisoners. Behind barbed-wire fences, each prisoner was issued leather service shoes with new laces and refurbished soles, a cap and two cotton field hats. Each also received socks, handkerchiefs, underwear, two pairs of pants, a web belt, a toothbrush, a shaving brush, a safety razor with five blades, a canteen cup, a fork, a knife, a spoon and dog tags stamped with his name, rank and serial number. Outer clothing came stamped with the six-inch yellow letters "PW" on front and back. Green and white sleeve patches were inscribed in bold letters: ITALY. Italian POWs received rosaries, a small statue of the Virgin Mary and a card bearing her image.

All foreign prisoners came under the jurisdiction of a newly created provost marshal general post. The provost marshal general brought all aspects of army law enforcement under a single office. Prison compounds were built where surplus barracks or obsolete Civilian Conservation Corps buildings were available. Where surplus barracks were not available, Provost Marshal General Allen Gullion was authorized to order construction of new compounds. In January 1942, the army paid $4 million for five hundred acres of land north of the Gila River. Blueprints were drafted for a sprawling complex, including barracks, a bakery, a 486-bed hospital, a swimming pool, theaters, volleyball and basketball courts and guard towers.

Arizona Rotarians warned Congress that the region's four large copper mines would be threatened by the presence of a POW camp. By the fall of 1942, military police escort companies were living in the barracks, training for the day when Nazi, Fascist and Japanese prisoners would arrive in the Arizona desert. Events in North Africa, however, accelerated their timetable. On May 7, 1943, British tanks rolled into Tunis and the Americans entered Bizerte. During April and May, a quarter million German and Italian soldiers walked out with their hands up. Thousands were placed in the ballast holds of vessels bound for the United States. Before long, Camp Florence was filled to capacity.[8]

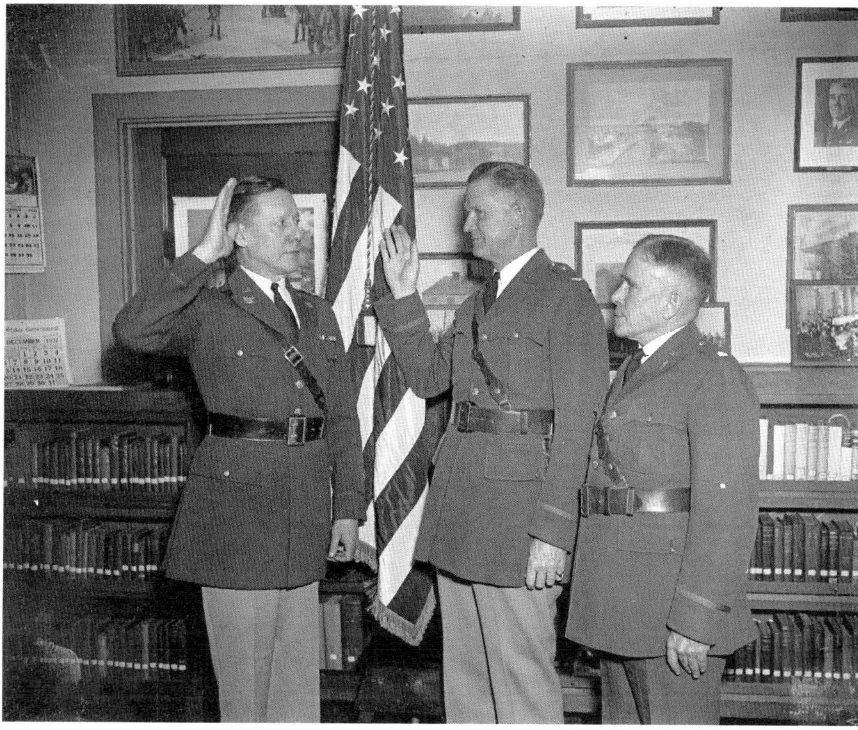

Major General Allen Gullion, judge advocate general (*left*), administering the oath of office to the new chief of chaplains, December 23, 1937, Washington, D.C. *Courtesy Library of Congress.*

The Italians were pawns in Benito Mussolini's dream of a new Roman Empire.[9] They had been conscripted with no training, no uniforms and no weapons. Their shoes were full of holes and their heads were full of lice. Hot, searing winds brought sand storms. Their meals consisted of carrots, salted sardines and moldy black bread. Italian soldiers detested their German allies and their own officers, who had little military skill.

Camp Florence welcomed its first Italian prisoners of war on May 4, 1943. Prisoners were given a sheet of stationery with space for name, rank and POW number and a space for a letter to a loved one in Italy. POW letters were gathered each day and given to censors. Any material deemed seditious was confiscated. At Camp Florence, censors found little to edit. Prisoners were happy with their camp and anxious for news from home.

Prisoners arrived in tattered uniforms, their skin blistered by the sun. Each man was given a physical exam, a dental checkup and an inoculation against smallpox. Personal items, such as watches, crucifixes and photographs, were

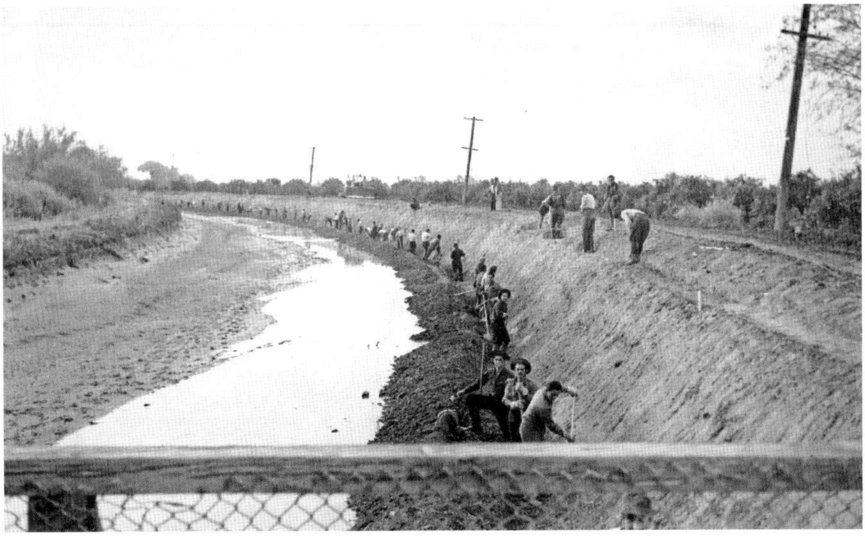

Italian prisoners of war from Camp Florence, Arizona, cleaning out the canals. *Courtesy Library of Congress.*

inventoried, and foreign currency was confiscated and supposedly returned to them later. Every prisoner was photographed, fingerprinted and issued a POW serial number. Although Mussolini had been running Italy, King Vittorio Emanuele III remained nominally in power. The War Department viewed Fascist sympathizers as troublemakers, and arriving prisoners were interviewed by an army intelligence officer.

Independent inspectors toured the compound and filed reports with the Red Cross and the YMCA. Their reports were complimentary: "Camp is spotlessly clean and sanitary." "Prisoner morale is good." "Florence is the nearest to a model camp which we have seen in POW camps."[10] Inmates painted a fresco in the camp chapel and built an adobe shell as an acoustic backdrop for evening concerts. Chester Hanson of the *Los Angeles Times* reported that a trio of opera singers wore white jackets sewn from bedsheets and bow ties cut from cardboard. Beautiful cigarette cases were made out of aluminum and polished with sand and a piece of bacon rind.[11] Vegetable gardens sprang up between the barracks. Prisoners found a letter on their mattress from the camp commander, Colonel William A. Holden, who would later serve as camp commander at Camp Papago Park:

> *To the Italian Prisoners of War, Florence Internment Camp Florence, Arizona: permit me to welcome you to this camp. Due to the fortunes*

> *of war, you find yourselves detained by the Army of the United States of America. Your detention will be managed strictly in accordance with agreements made between the United States of America and the Kingdom of Italy. You have my full assurance that you will at all times be humanely treated and protected, particularly against acts of violence, insults and public curiosity.*[12]

Holden urged the prisoners to take advantage of the opportunities to write home, participate in athletics, keep themselves and their quarters clean, obey all orders and instructions of the American army personnel and attend church services.[13]

At the Pentagon, the military planned for the invasion at Normandy. The U.S. Army now numbered 6 million compared to a prewar level of 100,000. The exodus of able-bodied workers from rural communities triggered a farm labor crisis throughout Arizona and Middle America. The Geneva Convention endorsed the use of POW labor for cultivating and harvesting crops. Italians were permitted to live near the farms in quarters not surrounded by barbed wire. However, harvesting cotton was hard work. Lower-grade cotton was picked by plucking the entire boll and then slipping handfuls into a long bag strapped over one shoulder. Higher-grade long-staple and short-staple cotton had to be separated with the fingers, an activity that left sore, raw hands and backs and aching shoulders from carrying heavy canvas bags. After the cotton was harvested, POWs cleaned irrigation ditches, dug potatoes, picked fruit and vegetables, harvested alfalfa and maintained roads. Farmers paid forty cents an hour for prisoner use. Camp work included the bakery, laundry, warehouse and mess halls. All prisoners earned ten cents a day whether they worked or not. Those who held jobs were paid an additional seventy cents a day. When the Italian government officially surrendered in September 1943, the Italian prisoners wanted to go home.

Prisoners began accusing American soldiers of stealing personal items. Officially, President Franklin Roosevelt classified Italy as a "co-belligerent" because U.S. soldiers still risked their lives to help liberate the Italians' homeland. On December 14, 1943, Marshal Pietro Badoglio, Italy's provisional leader, issued a statement to be read to all Italian prisoners of war in America: "It is our intention to proffer the Allies all possible, active collaboration in order to achieve the common objective of ridding our country of the residue of German troops still occupying a large section of our nation. It is therefore our duty to help the Allies in every possible way, excepting in actual combat."[14]

On January 6, 1944, the War Department's Army Special Forces drafted a plan that called for the formation of Italian Service Units, or ISUs. Qualified prisoners volunteered for military companies with enlisted men and officers. Members of ISUs were issued American army uniforms and wore Italian army rank insignias. Their pay was about twenty-four dollars per month.

CHAPTER 1
DAY OF INFAMY

In 1939, Columbia Pictures produced a film based on Clarence Kelland's book *Arizona*, set during the Civil War in Arizona Territory, at Old Tucson Studios near Tucson. The Fox Theatre, a grand Art Deco movie theater, was originally designed for vaudeville and silent movies. It was the site of the world premiere of the film *Arizona* starring William Holden and Jean Arthur. To economize during the Depression and onset of World War II, Columbia filmed the movie in black-and-white rather than color. By 1939, Americans were coming out of the Great Depression, but World War II was on the horizon. Adolf Hitler and his Nazis were wreaking devastation in Europe. His attack on Poland started World War II, and by 1941, Germany occupied much of Europe and North Africa. Japan saw its attack on Pearl Harbor as a preventive action to keep the U.S. Pacific Fleet from interfering with Japanese military actions in Southeast Asia against overseas territories belonging to Europe and the United States. Arizona's contribution to the war effort included new airbases, resulting in the birth of Arizona's aviation and manufacturing industries. After the war, the state experienced a population explosion when many veterans returned to live permanently in Arizona. World War II became a watershed in Arizona history, separating its existence as a Wild West frontier from a state with cities making use of the latest technical innovations.

Arizona was chosen to house prison camps for Japanese, Italians and Germans because its mild climate facilitated compliance with rules of the 1929 Geneva Convention. While its warm winter climate was pleasant enough, nothing was

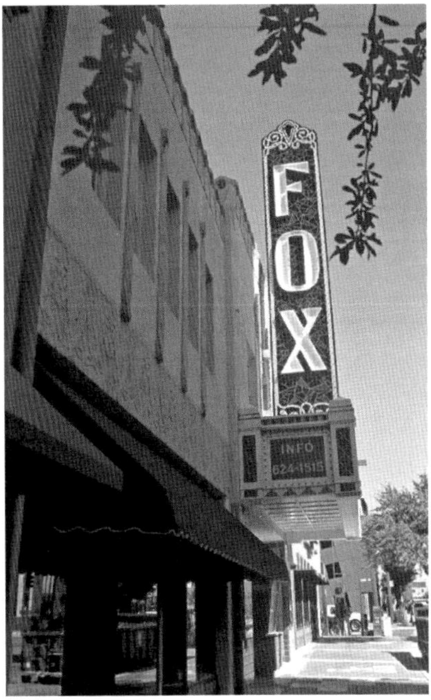

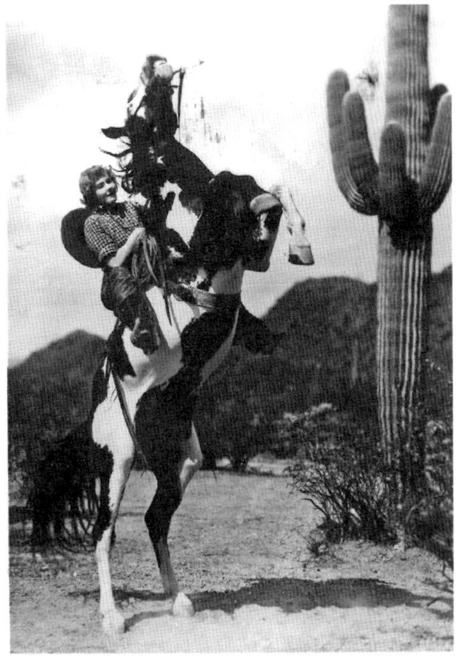

Left: The beautiful old Fox Theatre has been restored to its glory days. *Courtesy Tucson Chamber of Commerce.*

Right: Jean Arthur starring in the movie *Arizona*. *Courtesy Old Tucson Studios.*

stipulated about keeping prisoners cool in the summer. However, it was the courage of its people that really marked the state. Lieutenant Colonel Barry Goldwater, a future senator and Republican presidential nominee, forced his way into military service in spite of his poor eyesight, and Arizona politician Ernest William McFarland is considered to be a father of the GI Bill, which provided education for Arizona veterans. He is the only Arizonan to serve in all three branches of Arizona government—two at the state level, one at the federal level. He was a democratic senator from Arizona from 1941 to 1953 (majority leader from 1951 to 1953) before serving as the tenth governor of Arizona from 1955 to 1959. Finally, McFarland sat as chief justice on the Arizona Supreme Court in 1968.

Eight Arizonans perished on the day of infamy during the terrible explosion on the USS *Arizona* at Pearl Harbor at Hawaii. Communications was a problem, but Japanese cryptographers had become adept at breaking military codes, which resulted in extensive loss of American lives. Philip Johnston, a civil engineer who had lived on the Navajo Indian Reservation, where his parents were missionaries, spoke Navajo with his playmates. He introduced the idea of the Navajo code talkers to the military, and a code book was developed for new initiates. At the Battle of Iwo Jima, Major Howard Connor had six Navajo code talkers working around the clock during the first two days of the battle. These six marines sent and received over eight hundred messages. Ira Hayes, a Pima Indian, would help the marines raise the flag on Mount Suribachi.[15] Hayes, never comfortable with his fame, descended into alcoholism after his service. He died of exposure to cold and alcoholism after a night of drinking on January 23, 1955, and was buried with full military honors at Arlington National Cemetery on February 2, 1955.

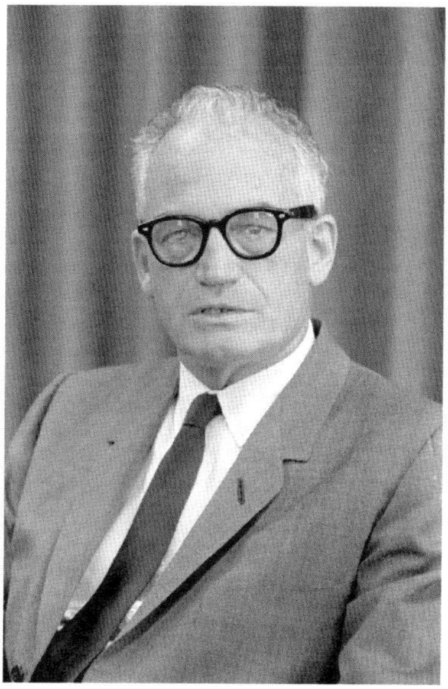

Senator Barry Goldwater was a long-term Arizona politician and World War II pilot. *Courtesy Library of Congress.*

During World War II, air bases sprang up all over southern Arizona. Fort Huachuca had been created in the 1880s when soldiers arrived to protect settlers from Geronimo and his Apaches. It became the home of the buffalo soldiers and during World War II was staffed with black WAACs (Women's Army Auxiliary Corps). Arizona women also played important roles in the Red Cross, both on the homefront and abroad.

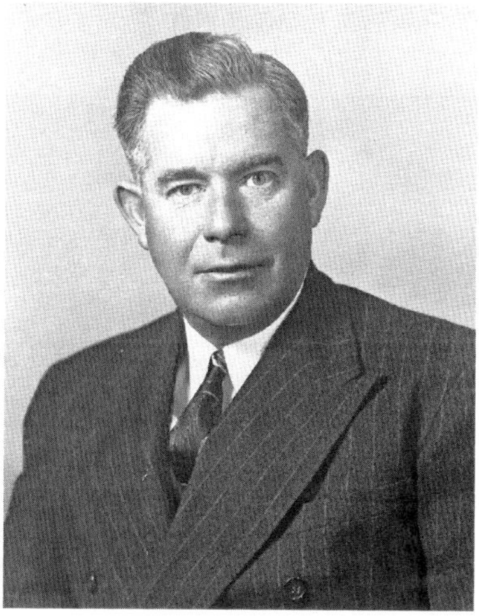

Congressman Ernest McFarland was instrumental in getting the GI Bill of Education passed. *Courtesy U.S. Senate Historical Office.*

Almost immediately after the bombing of Pearl Harbor, the Hawaiian consular staff was transferred to the Triangle T Ranch in southern Arizona. An Italian POW camp was set up near Florence, Arizona, and Camp Florence welcomed its first Italian prisoners of war on May 4, 1943.

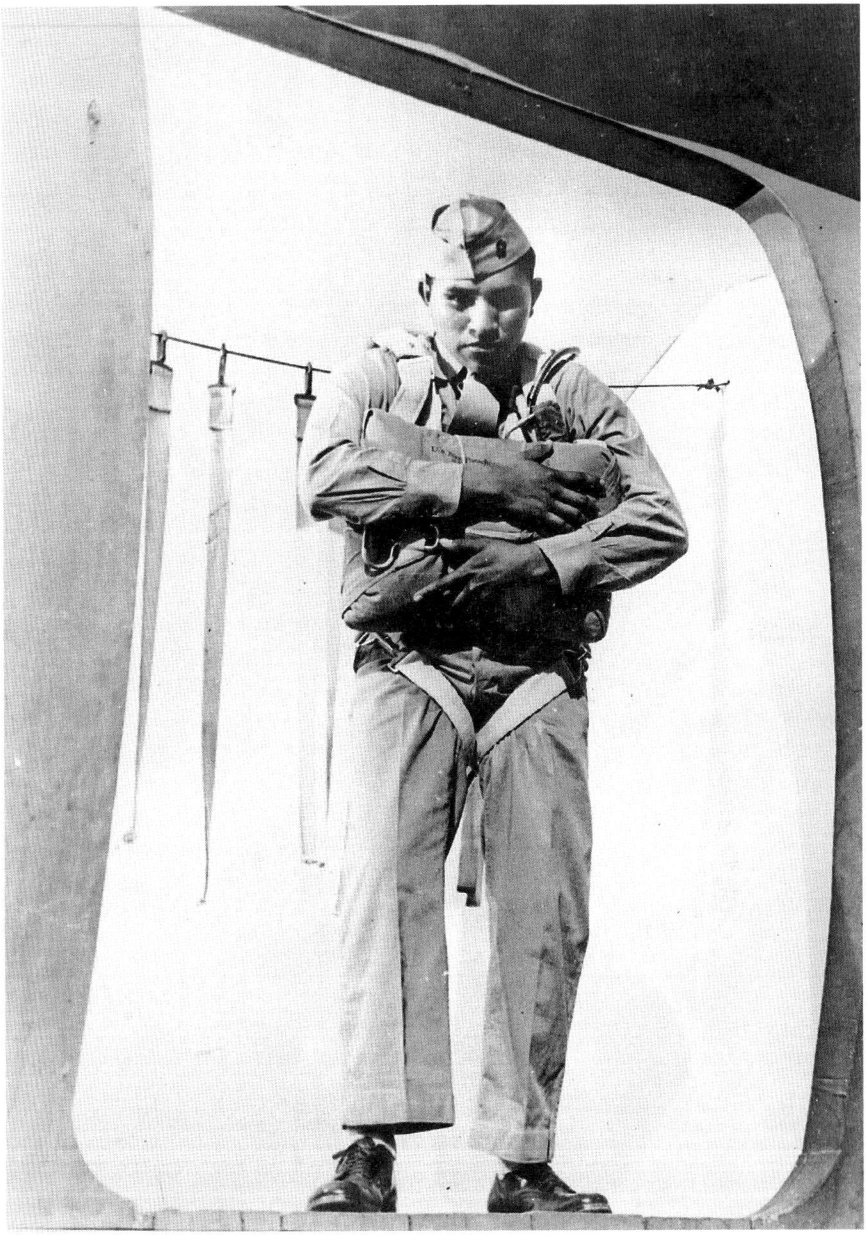

Ira Hayes was an Arizona Pima Indian who helped raise the flag at Mount Suribachi. *Courtesy Library of Congress.*

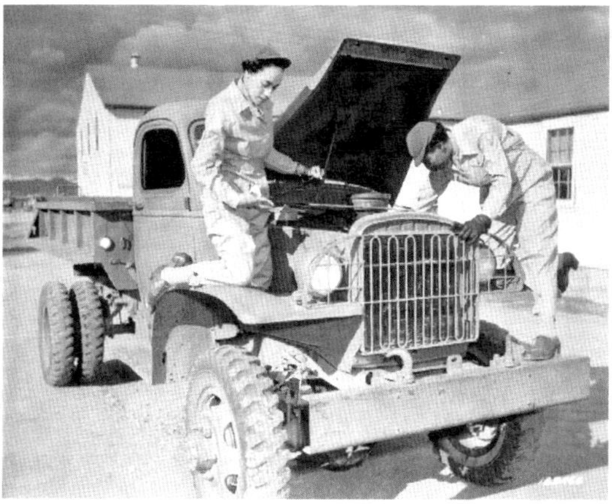

Left: The all-black Women's Auxiliary Army Corps was responsible for the maintenance of military equipment at Fort Huachuca during World War II. *Courtesy Fort Huachuca Military Museum.*

Below: The destruction of the USS *Arizona* marks the day of infamy, December 7, 1941. *Courtesy Library of Congress.*

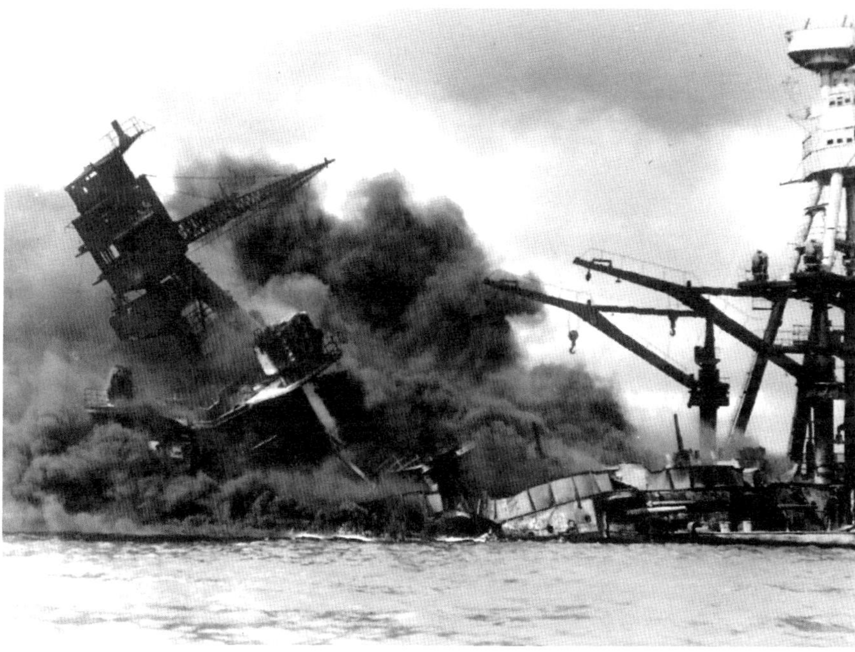

Both the army and the local farmers were desperate for manpower. The Italians performed menial labor, freeing American soldiers for military duty; but at the same time, Arizonans were uncomfortable because they lived near sensitive military operations. While the army tried to separate hardcore fascists, it was difficult because they intimidated POWs. The War Department decided that all POWs would have to be rescreened, and the Fascists were banned from Italian Service Units (ISUs). Camp Florence was considered to be the best example of how POWs anywhere should be treated.

On May 1, 1944, Captain Francis Beckman of Seattle arrived to take charge of the Twenty-Eighth Italian Service Unit, which would be based at Seattle's Fort Lawton. The companies were assembled by combining soldiers with a mix of useful skills. More than two hundred men—thousands of miles from home, sick with worry about their families after years of fruitless battle, anxious about an unknown future for an uncertain period of time—were leaving Florence. On May 18, the train pulled out along the Southern Pacific spur at 4:38 p.m.[16]

Japanese Americans, whether born in the United States or in Japan, were rounded up and sent to internment camps for the duration of the war. The internment forced relocation and incarceration of approximately 120,000 people. President Roosevelt ordered this incarceration shortly after the attack on Pearl Harbor. Members of the Japanese diplomatic corps were held at the Hampstead in New Hampshire until they could be repatriated. The exception was the Honolulu consular staff, which was held at the Triangle T Ranch in southern Arizona. These were the Japanese who had given the orders about when and where to drop the bombs on Pearl Harbor. In 1929, the Triangle T had come into the possession of Catherine Tutt as the result of a breach of a contract to marry suit. She designed the buildings we see today and named it the Triangle T. Dignitaries including John F. Kennedy, General John "Black Jack" Pershing, the Rockefellers and the Vanderbilts stayed at the ranch.

At Honolulu, U.S. naval personnel could only stare in horror as the blazing battleship USS *Arizona* emerged through the clouds of the Pearl Harbor inferno on Sunday morning, December 7, 1941. At their headquarters, Japanese officials listened to the radio above the crescendo of exploding torpedoes and bombs. Twice they heard three words: "East Wind, Rain," in what was otherwise a routine weather report. This phrase signaled that Japan had gone to war with the United States. They knew that their country was ready to sacrifice them and that they would be arrested and probably killed by the Americans. They could not have known that they would spend four months at the Triangle T guest ranch in southern Arizona. When the Federal Bureau of Investigation (FBI) arrived at the consulate, Honolulu police captain Benjamin Van Kuren had already stopped the Japanese from burning coded documents. Consul Nagao Kita and Vice-Consul Otojiro Okuda knew that Pearl Harbor would be attacked but not the exact date, and so they had arranged to play golf on December 7. Their cab driver arrived and was told that his services would not be required. No mention was made of a later date. For many months, the United States had suspected

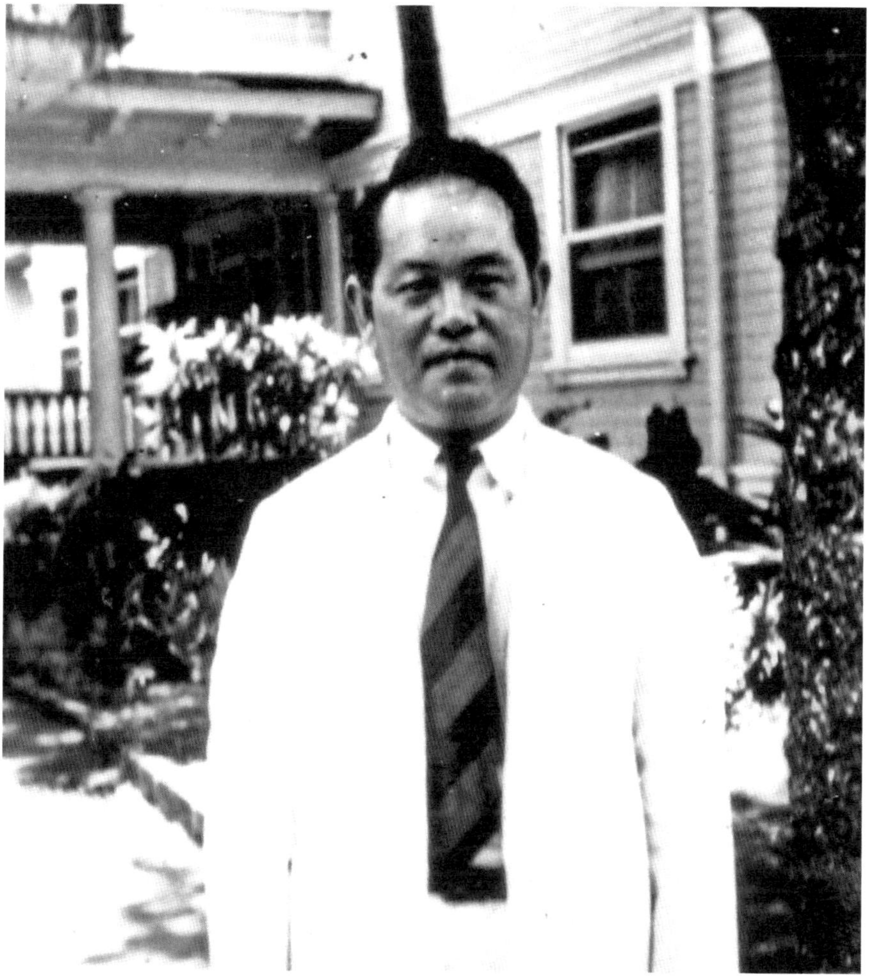

Consul Nagao Kita and Vice-Consul Otojiro Okuda knew that Pearl Harbor would be attacked but not the exact date, and so they had arranged to play golf on December 7. *Courtesy National Archives, Washington, D.C.*

the Japanese consulate in Honolulu of espionage. The 400 *toritsuginin*, or "persons able to handle matters," and 730 Japanese language schoolteachers in Hawaii had no consular status but were by reason of intellect and education ideal for espionage.[17]

The late Rhea Robinson recalled the day when a U.S. Border Patrol agent told her husband, Reed P. Robinson, to be ready to go on assignment in thirty minutes. Weeks later, she received a letter from him, postmarked El Paso. She did not know that he had been on a special detail at the Triangle

T, just twenty minutes down the road from their home in Benson.[18]

In Hawaii, the officials of the Japanese consulate remained under house arrest until they were placed in the custody of the U.S. Navy. When they arrived at San Pedro, California, Robinson and border patrol agents guarded the entourage in air-conditioned Pullman staterooms to Dragoon, Arizona, where they were transferred to the Triangle T. State Department special agent Thomas F. Fitch had been given forty-eight hours to find accommodations for the Japanese. He and Arizona postal inspector Harry H. Smith scouted Arizona and settled on the Triangle T. In the spirit of patriotism, Smith used his own transportation so there would be no charge to the government. This operation was shrouded in secrecy because no harm must come to these prisoners if an exchange for Americans in Japan was to be negotiated. All in all, twenty-three consulate members included Nagao Kita, consul general; Otojiro Okuda, vice-consul general, his wife, Sadako, and their children Kazuhiro and Masahiro; Sainon Tsukikawa, consul secretary; Kyonosuke Yuge, consul secretary, his wife, Kiyoko, and their daughters Kazuko and Ayako; Kohichi Seki, consul secretary, and his wife, Michiko; Takeo Yoshikawa, aka Tadasi Morimura, chancellor; Kita's servants, Takeo and Hana Kusanobu; Setsuko Yamada, Okuda's maid; Sadako Kojima, maid; Saburo Sumida, gardener, his wife, Kaneyo, and their two sons, Robert Hiroyoshi and Herman Minoru; and Rokuro Fukushima, gardener, and his wife, Teruo.

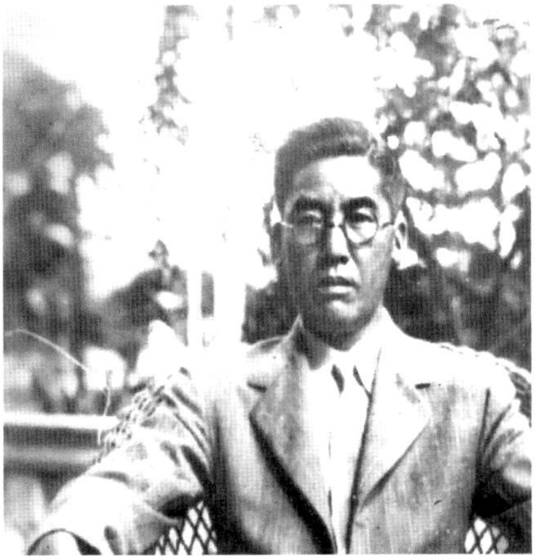

Otojiro Okuda served as consul in Hawaii until Pearl Harbor Day, when he was captured and sent to the Triangle T Ranch in Arizona. *Courtesy National Archives, Washington, D.C.*

On April 15, 1942, FBI agent Fred G. Tillman arrived at the Triangle T to interview the Japanese. Tillman, an Asian expert, received an appointment from General Douglas MacArthur to serve with Army Counter Intelligence Corps while stationed at Manila. Tillman worked with the corps' internal security section on postwar Japanese. Ultimately, he would participate in the Pearl Harbor hearings in Washington.

At the Triangle T, separated by barbed-wire fence, Tillman was not allowed to interrogate the Japanese until his request had cleared with the

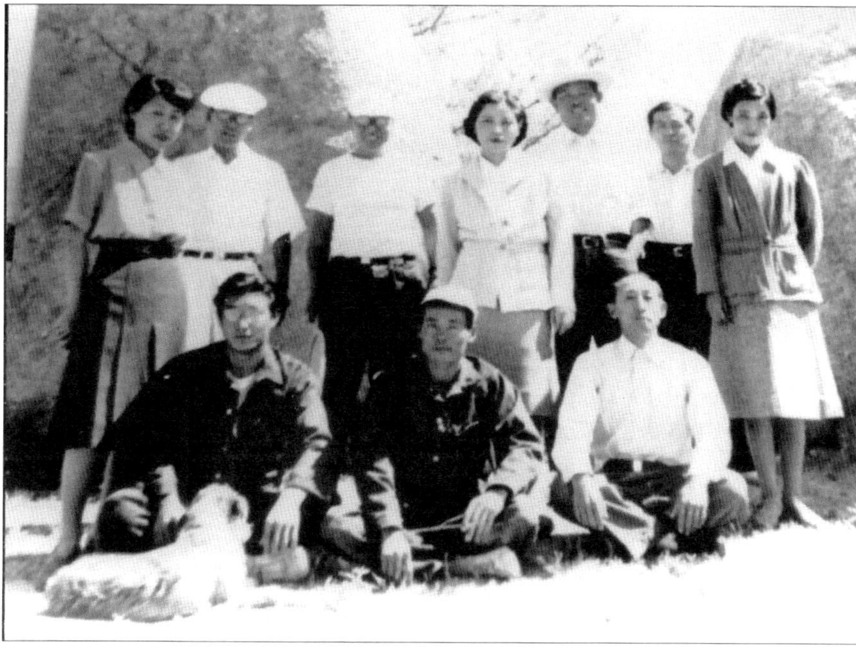

The Japanese consulate from Hawaii at the Triangle T Ranch in Arizona. *Courtesy the late Rhea Robinson.*

State Department. President Roosevelt wanted to keep Consul General Nagao Kita incommunicado from the other diplomats. Kita served nineteen years with the Japanese Foreign Office. A widower devoted to his work, the affable, stocky diplomat enjoyed golf. Kita described his duties as routine consular work. Otojiro Okuda served as consul until Kita arrived. It was a breach of protocol that he did not notify the U.S. State Department when his duties officially terminated on June 25, 1941, serious because he no longer had diplomatic immunity. He remained at the consulate, presumably to commit espionage. At Dragoon, he refused to discuss consular business but became very "agitated" when Tillman pointed out his lack of credentials. J. Edgar Hoover sought permission to prosecute him, but Assistant Secretary of State Adolph Berle responded, "Quite likely the Japanese consul deserves to be shot but we should undeniably risk the life of one of our men, without gaining very much save abstract justice." Okuda refused to discuss his visits to Pearl Harbor with a spy, Takeo Yoshikawa, or his association with a German Nazi, Otto Kuehn. He admitted giving Yoshikawa a package but said that he did not know that it contained $14,000. On or about October 25, 1941, Kita asked Kuehn to obtain facts and figures on the U.S. Navy. Yoshikawa followed Kita to Honolulu on March 27, 1941, after serving two years with the Foreign Service.[19]

The Japanese spy slipped past U.S. authorities under the alias Tadasi Morimura. He knew every ship in the American fleet. Yoshikawa possessed the absolute unquestioning loyalty of the samurai and the discipline of a Buddhist. His real identity was not known to his colleagues. Because of his evasion of consular work and frequent absenteeism, he incurred staff resentment. The handsome twenty-nine-year-old spy associated with geishas at the Shuncho-ro Tea House. From the second floor of Shuncho-ro, Yoshikawa observed Pearl Harbor and Hickam Field through a telescope. Colonel George W. Bicknell recalled, "He [Yoshikawa] and his taxi driver were all over the goddamn place." At Dragoon, Tillman observed that Yoshikawa's left ring finger had been amputated at the first joint, indicating that he was a member of the Black Dragon Society (Kokuryu Kai), a group that severed its members' fingers for identification. Treasurer Kohichi Seki studied law at the Meiji University. From unrestricted areas, he photographed Pearl Harbor, and the Americans could do nothing about it.

Kyonosuke Yuge, a consulate secretary, was fluent in Korean and English. Sainon Tsukikawa, a Foreign Service employee, lived at the consulate until Yoshikawa arrived, at which time he moved into a hotel. Saburo Sumida, listed as a gardener, entered Hawaii on February 15, 1937. Two of his Hawaiian-born children resided at the Triangle T, but the other two lived in Japan. Sumida had been awarded the Foreign Minister's Wooden Cup for meritorious service in the overseas development of the Japanese Empire—a most unusual award for a gardener. Sumida's son Robert Hiroyoshi told Tillman that he was studying "electricity and radio" at the Honolulu Vocational School.

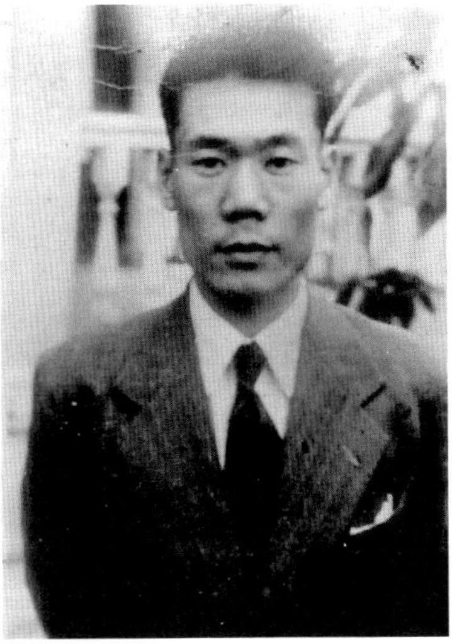

Tadasi Morimura knew every ship in the American fleet. Yoshikawa possessed the absolute unquestioning loyalty of the samurai and the discipline of a Buddhist. *Courtesy National Archives, Washington, D.C.*

The U.S. government paid the Triangle T $900 per week for room and board for the Japanese, $225 for the border patrol guards and $35 for tips. In addition, the State Department remitted $100 from its Confidential Fund to Kita for incidentals.

When the Japanese consulate arrived at San Pedro, California, on February 17, State Department special agent Edward Bailey had assumed responsibility for their welfare. The Japanese received their personal mail after it passed U.S. censors. Twice a week, Bailey took their lists, which he said "read like a Sears Roebuck catalogue," to Tucson, where he did their shopping.

On May 21, 1942, the State Department ordered Bailey to prepare the Japanese for repatriation. A few days later, the prisoners boarded two Pullmans at Dragoon and, under the border patrol guards, including Reed Robinson, traveled to New Jersey. On June 7, Japanese from the United States, Canada and Latin America began arriving in New York City for repatriation. They were housed in the Pennsylvania Hotel, where border patrol agents and New York City police guarded all entrances to the top two floors. On Thursday, June 18, 1942, the enemy aliens were boarded for Japan on the neutral Swedish ship *Gripsholm*.

Almost overnight, southern Arizona became a training ground for soldiers destined to fight overseas. Administrators turned their attention to constructing Nazi POW camps, which were not of the quality of Camp Florence, and there were frequent escape attempts, beatings, murder and mayhem. An undermanned staff was charged with guarding approximately 4,000 rebellious foreign prisoners under the psychological and physical control of zealous Nazi officers. The U.S. Army assumed responsibility for the custody of all foreign prisoners. On the East Coast, prisoners were processed through Fort George G. Meade in Washington, D.C., and sent on to Fort Hunt at Alexandria, Virginia, for interrogation. West Coast prisoners were processed at Angel Island, California, before being transferred to the Fort Tracy interrogation center. By the end of 1942, the United States had 1,881 prisoners; a year later, it detained 172,879 captives. By 1945, the United States' total prisoner of war population had risen to 371,683 Germans, 50,273 Italians and 3,915 Japanese. These prisoners did not include incarcerated civilians who were suspected of operating as enemy aliens.

During 1940, German U-boats had sunk 217 Allied vessels with their wolfpacks, a concept devised by Admiral Karl Doenitz to use submarines to overcome the convoy defenses. Doenitz, born on September 16, 1891, near Berlin, entered the Imperial Naval Academy in 1910 as a cadet and six years later was promoted to lieutenant and transferred to the U-boat service. By 1918, he had become commander of *U-25* and later of *U-68*. In 1928, he commanded a torpedo boat, and in 1935, he was transferred to the Weddingen U-boat flotilla *Neustadt*. In 1939, he was promoted to rear

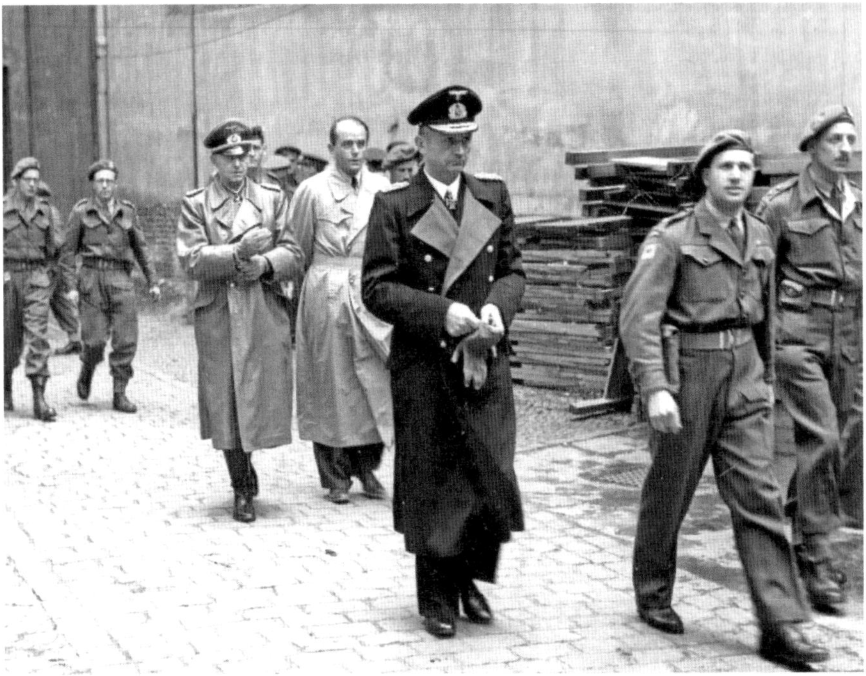

Admiral Karl Doenitz being turned over to the British after World War II. *Courtesy Library of Congress.*

admiral and appointed commander in chief of the U-boats. In 1942, he was supreme commander of the German navy. In May 1945, with Hitler's suicide, he took over Hitler's position as head of the government and sued for an armistice. The wolfpack concept was put into effect as soon as sufficient numbers of submarines were available and was quite successful. In the early stages of the war, the U-boats effectively destroyed Allied shipping. German U-boats hunted in "wolfpacks," where multiple submarines stayed close together, making it easier to sink a specific target. Because speed and range were severely limited under water while running on battery power, U-boats spent most of their time above surface running on diesel engines, diving only when attacked.

The summer of 1942 saw the end of the Allied hunting season. During June, the Germans had torpedoed 145 Allied ships. This devastation ended when the Allies provided escorted convoys, coastal blackouts and patrol planes.

CHAPTER 2

DIVEBOMB TO HELL

By 1944, the Great Depression and World War II had taken a heavy toll on Arizona and the rest of the nation. Still, Americans believed that the end was in sight, and hope soared when the government lifted meat rationing. Women composed 42 percent of the West Coast aircraft labor force. A sense of the country's mood could be found in the Hit Parade songs "Accentuate the Positive," "Don't Fence Me In" and "Swinging on a Star." John Van Druten gave us the sentimental stage play *I Remember Mama*. The most popular movie, *Going My Way*, starred crooner Bing Crosby. Martin Flavin received the Pulitzer Prize for his *Journey in the Dark*, a melancholy chronicle of a son seeking to understand his father. Despite protests that the International Red Cross charged Allied soldiers for coffee, sweaters and other items, the organization received the Nobel Peace Prize. That year, the Cardinals won the World Series against the Browns, and Army trounced Navy. Times were hard, but Americans found ways to have fun and indulge in a little silliness.

The seven young German prisoners accused of murdering Werner Drechsler and their victim had all been born in Germany's bleak years after World War I. Their education began in public schools, where they were exposed to intense indoctrination under Hitler's Youth Movement. Hitler bragged to his opposition that if he did not have them, he had their children. They had been drilled with these words:

We are the rollicking Hitler Youth;
We have no need for Christian truth;

No evil old priest these ties can sever
We're Hitler's children now and ever.

Their lives shared common threads with that of their victim, Werner Drechsler. Enlisted U-boat men were steelworkers and mechanics, with only a basic elementary education plus a few years of trade school. All had survived devastating bomb and torpedo attacks. All had seen many of their comrades die terrible deaths in the last harrowing moments of an attack.

"U-boat" is an anglicized version of the German word U-boot, an abbreviation of *unterseeboot*, or "undersea boat." The term refers specifically to military submarines operated by Germany during World Wars I and II, which effectively enforced a naval blockade against enemy shipping. The primary targets of the U-boat campaigns were the merchant convoys transporting supplies among the Soviet Union and the Allied territories in the Mediterranean. The Treaty of Versailles had limited the size of Germany's surface navy.

Werner Drechsler, who loved submarines but hated Hitler, turned traitor to Germany and provided military information to the Allies. His seven executioners, their youthful faces already set in grim determination, revealed nothing more upon capture than name, rank and serial number. They professed allegiance to Hitler, but as enlisted men, it is doubtful if they qualified as party members. To join the party, pure Aryan lineage had to be proved several generations back. The American Office of Naval Intelligence interrogated prisoners regarding German military strategy, scientific information, industrial data, names of spies and tactical intelligence. Interrogators found it difficult to distinguish which prisoners held sincere anti-Nazi sentiments and which ones only paid lip service to anti-Nazism. Opportunists saw the last Reich as an empire gasping its final breaths, and they wanted to be on the winning side. Other prisoners, such as Drechsler, were, by conviction, anti-Nazi. The military attempted to protect anti-Nazi prisoners by quartering them in different camps. However, Camp Papago Park incarcerated both Nazis and anti-Nazis and made little effort to segregate the two groups.

Otto Stengel, the only married member of the executioners and the oldest submariner, never saw his wife and two children, a son and a daughter, after he left Germany. Twelve years after his execution, his wife, Anna, filed for a special pension for herself and their children on the grounds that Stengel had died an "unlawful" death.[20] Born in Aunkofen, the Stengel family moved to Munich while Otto was still a baby. After eight years in public school and three years in a trade school, he went to work as a locksmith. In 1939, Stengel enlisted in the German navy, and two years later, he joined the crew of the *U-352.*

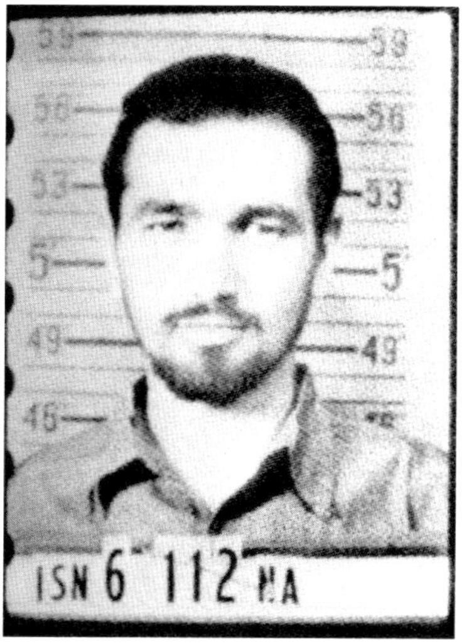

Otto Stengel (*U-352*), the only married member of the executioners and the oldest submariner, celebrated his twenty-sixth birthday on death row at Fort Leavenworth on February 9, 1945. *Courtesy National Archives, Washington, D.C.*

Stengel's submarine survived several Allied attacks before it was captured. The USS *Icarus* spotted the *U-352* while it cruised near the North Carolina coast off Cape Lookout on May 9, 1942. When *Icarus* fired its torpedoes, *U-352* became the second German submarine to be sunk by the Americans. The thirty-two-year-old captain of the *U-352*, Hellmut Rathke, left his wife and daughter in Flensburg. His crew held him in high respect. The *Icarus* crew was criticized for fraternizing with the prisoners, claiming this hampered efforts to obtain information. The crew was allowed, however, to tune in to American radio programs in the boat. The *Icarus* made three attacks on the U-boat when it came to the surface.

The *Icarus* opened fire on the *U-352* with all its guns as soon as the conning tower broke the surface of the water. Members of the *U-352* crew escaped through its conning tower hatch. The only U-boat previously sunk on the East Coast had gone down with all hands, so there were no standing orders concerning the rescue of survivors. *Icarus* called both Norfolk and Charleston before receiving permission to pick up survivors. It was decided that aside from the humanitarian point of view, the rescue of the enemy could provide valuable information. Forty minutes later, *Icarus* picked up thirty-three members, including Otto Stengel. When the captain ordered the crew to abandon ship, Stengel dived into the cold water near Cape Lookout and swam until the *Icarus* picked him up. He refused to provide any information other than that allowed by the Geneva Convention. Stengel spent his years in captivity at various prisoner of war camps in Massachusetts, New Mexico and Oklahoma before his final transfer to Camp Papago Park. Five of the POWs were wounded: Gerhard Keussel lost a leg and died onboard ship, one POW fractured his left wrist, another lost his left

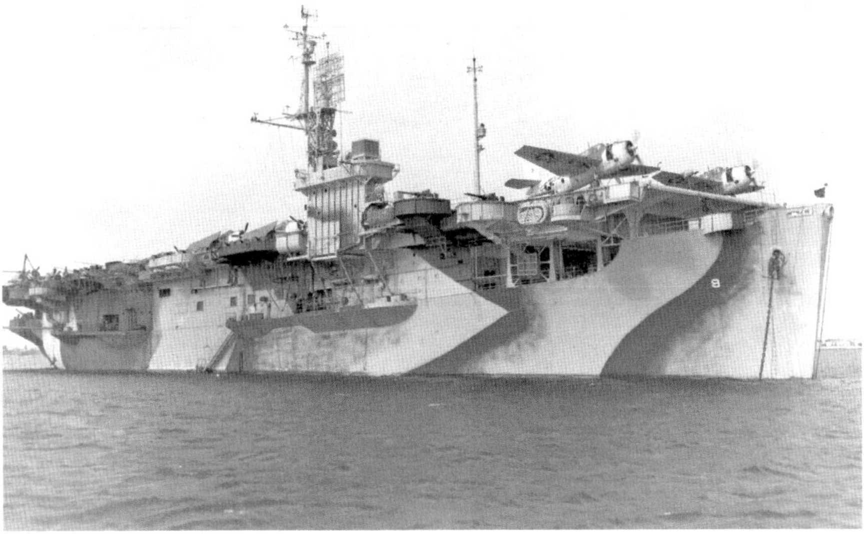

Drechsler's vessel, the *U-118*, had been at sea less than a month when it was attacked by two aircraft west of the Canary Islands, followed by eight planes from the carrier USS *Bogue*. *Courtesy of Captain Jerry Mason's (Retd.) U-boat Archive.*

arm and the other two were only slightly wounded. On arrival, the *U-352* officers and crew were interviewed. The Americans described them as small, healthy, loyal Germans, well disciplined in security and military in bearing and appearance. They came aboard the *Icarus* in order of seniority. Rathke complained about his treatment and assumed strict control of his men. He professed an unqualified admiration for Hitler, whom he described as a genius. When they left, Captain Rathke thanked the *Icarus*'s commanding officer, Lieutenant Maurice D. Jester, for the good treatment his crew had received. Jester became the first person to be awarded the Navy Cross for bravery in World War II.[21]

Of the seven accused submariners, Heinrich Ludwig spent the longest time as a prisoner of war. Ludwig, born twenty-five years earlier in Essen, grew up in the shadow of the Krupp steelworks. After eight years in a public school, he went to work for the Krupp mines in the Ruhr Valley. He received a military deferment because Germany considered Krupp work an essential labor position, but the patriotic Ludwig refused to be denied military service. In early 1942, he resigned his position with Krupp and formally enlisted in the German navy. Although undereducated even for an enlisted man, Ludwig succeeded in joining the crew of the *U-199* as an ordinary seaman. The *U-199*, under Captain Hans Werner Kraus, cast off

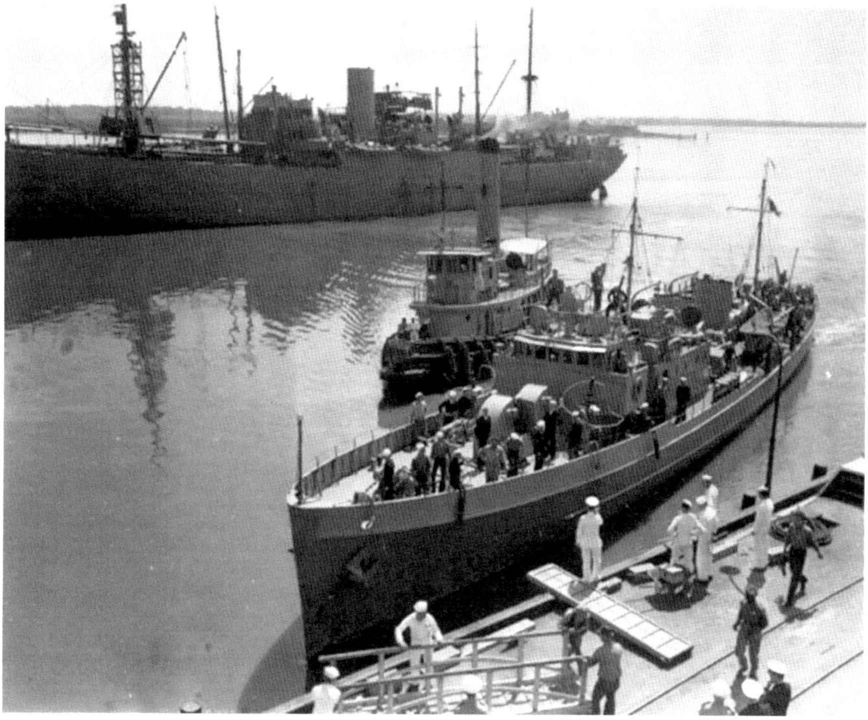

USCGC *Icarus* arrives at the Charleston Navy Yard on May 10, 1942, the day after sinking *U-352* and bringing in German survivors. *Courtesy of Captain Jerry Mason's (Retd.) U-boat Archive.*

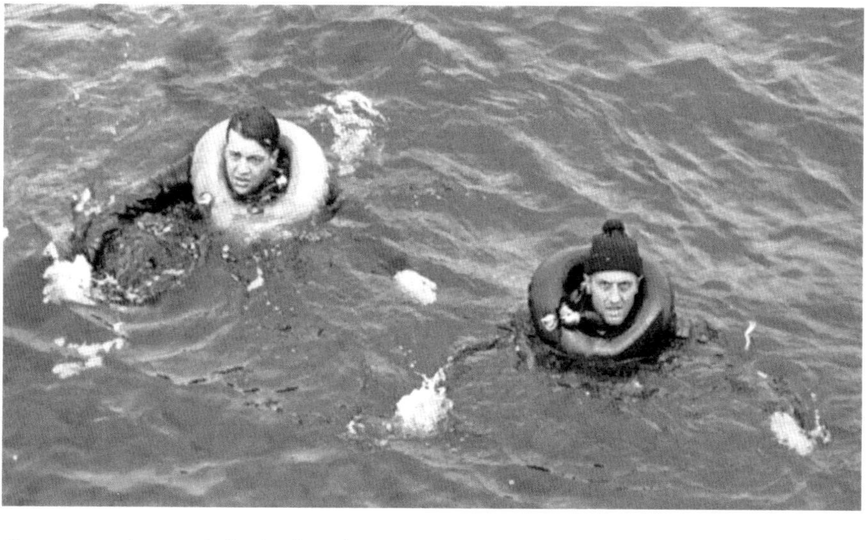

German survivors wait for the Americans to get permission to rescue them. *Courtesy of Captain Jerry Mason's (Retd.) U-boat Archive.*

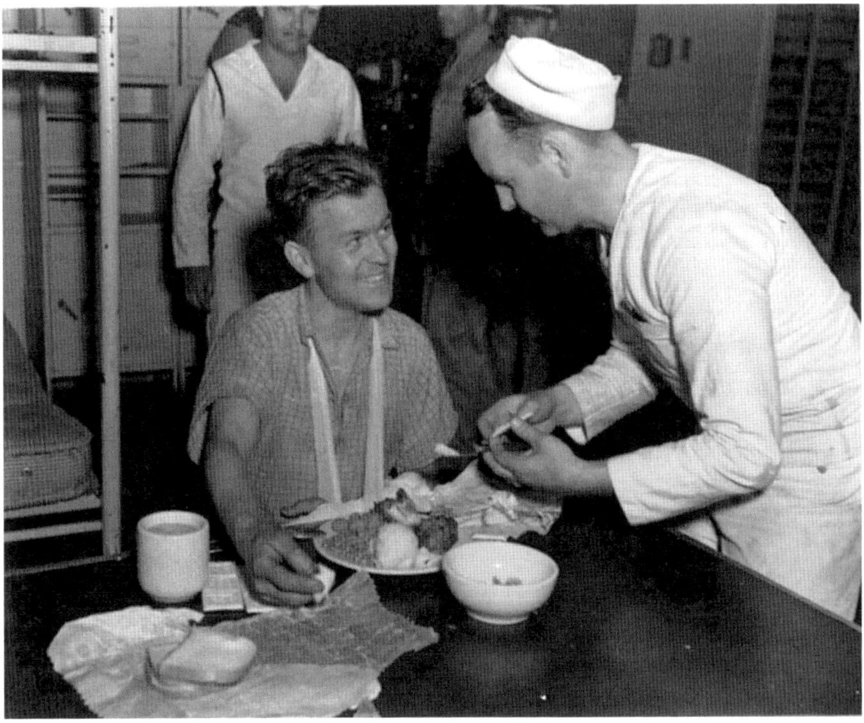

One day his ship is being blown up and he is wounded, and now he is eating mashed potatoes and fried chicken and his American captor is helping him butter his crackers. Life is good. *Courtesy of Captain Jerry Mason's (Retd.) U-boat Archive.*

on its only cruise on May 13, 1943. On June 25, a British plane spotted the submarine about one hundred miles north of Rio de Janeiro. A month later, the *U-199* unleashed its torpedoes at the British *Henzada* as it headed toward Santos, Brazil. All three torpedoes went wide of the mark. The submarine resurfaced and fired two more torpedoes. This time, the British ship broke in half and sank. That evening, the *U-199* crew enjoyed a victory celebration with a special dinner. Two days later, a Brazilian plane dropped six bombs on the *U-199*. The captain had no choice but to abandon ship. Although Ludwig emerged unharmed from the attack, only eleven of the ship's sixty-one-member crew survived. Survivors were interrogated and held briefly at a U.S. Navy base in Recifé, Brazil. From Recifé, Ludwig and his crew mates were flown to Miami, Florida. On August 18, 1943, eighteen days after his boat sank, the military transferred Ludwig to the processing center at Fort Meade, Maryland. Like Stengel, he steadfastly refused to give out any vital information. Ludwig shared a cell with another prisoner with a

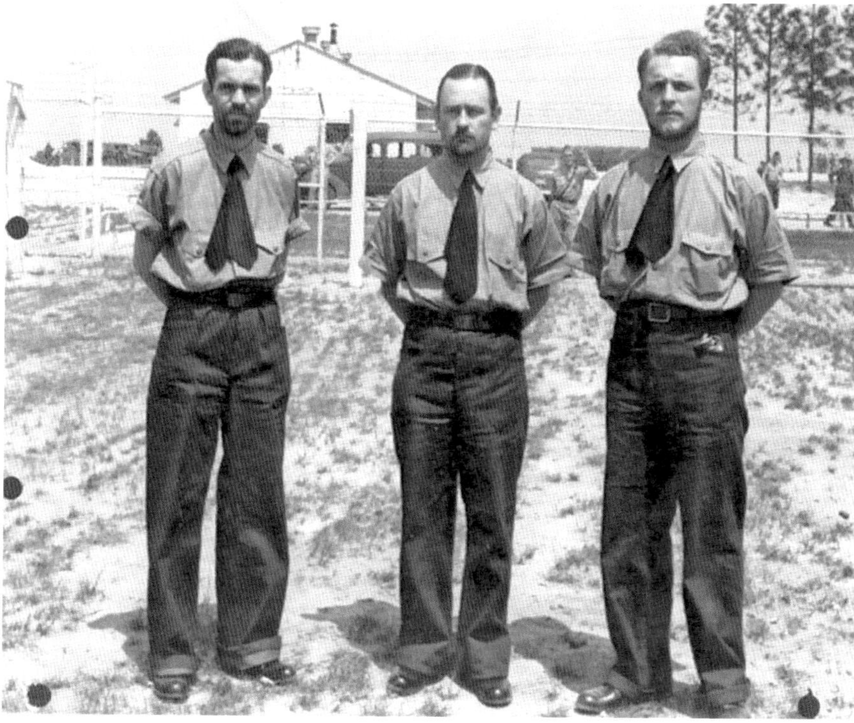

U-352 officers at Fort Bragg. *Left to right*: Lieutenant Ernst Kammerer, Captain Hellmut Rathke and Lieutenant Oskar Bernard. *Courtesy of Captain Jerry Mason's (Retd.) U-boat Archive.*

rank equivalent to a navy mate. Although he did not know it at the time, this would be his first meeting with Drechsler, who introduced himself as "Obermaat Limmer." Ludwig instinctively distrusted him.

Helmut Fischer, Fritz Franke, Guenther Kuelsen, Bernhard Reyak and Rolf Wizuy were shipmates on the *U-615*. Beginning in the North Atlantic on July 29, 1943, and ending on August 7 in the Caribbean, Captain Ralph Kapitzky of the *U-615* fought one of the longest naval battles of any U-boat against aircraft during the war. Although his boat was ultimately sunk by the USS *Walker*, the long-running battle absorbed the attention of the U.S. forces in the area and enabled the many other U-boats in the Caribbean to surface and escape. Kapitzky died while giving orders to defend the boat.

Helmut Fischer, a good-looking twenty-two-year-old submariner with wavy brown hair, was the ranking member of the group. Born and raised in Ravensburg in southern Germany, he completed public school, attended a

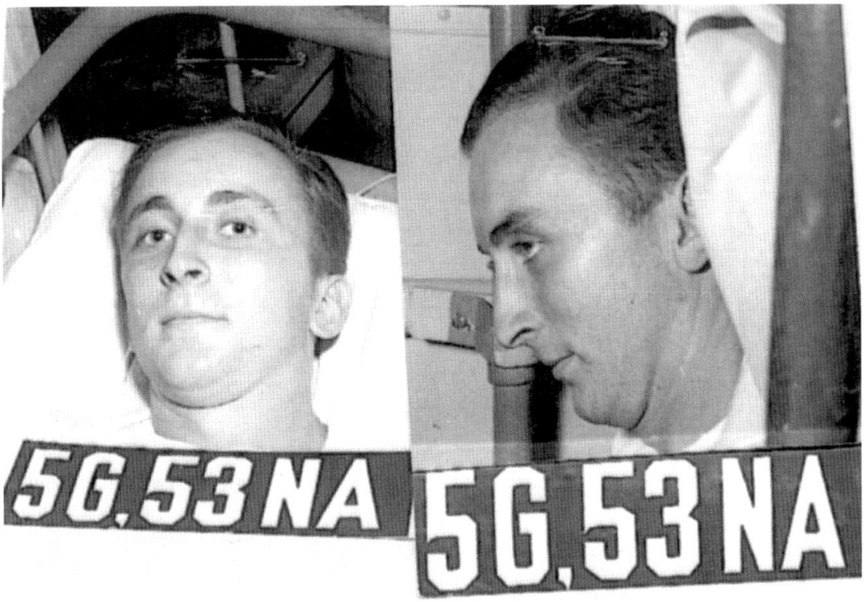

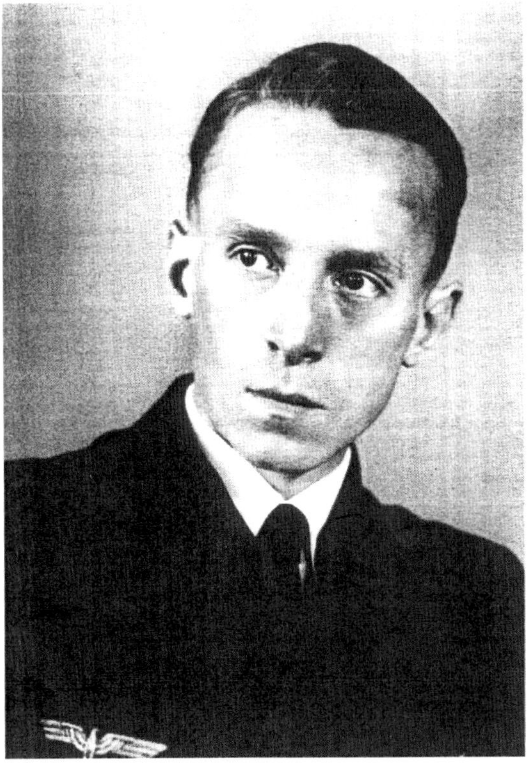

Above: Heinrich Ludwig, an ordinary seaman on the *U-199*, spent the longest time of Drechsler's seven executioners as a prisoner of war. *Courtesy National Archives, Washington, D.C.*

Left: During the sinking of the *U-615*, Captain Rolf Kapitzky was mortally wounded by machine gun fire and died after bidding farewell to his crew. *Courtesy of Captain Jerry Mason's (Retd.) U-boat Archive.*

trade school and joined the Hitler Youth group. After graduation, he worked as a tool and die maker. Dissatisfied with serving the war effort from a factory, Fischer enlisted in the German navy and qualified for U-boat service. He trained with the other crew members at Breda, Netherlands, where he met the youngest of the seven prisoners, Fritz Franke.

Franke carried only about 155 pounds on his six-foot frame. The cold, reserved Franke was the most resolute Nazi and least cooperative prisoner. Franke grew up in the industrial Frankfurt on the border with Poland. Franke studied to be a mechanic, but after three years in trade school, he joined the navy. He took the Hitler Youth Movement seriously and adapted easily to the rigid discipline and difficult U-boat training. Franke secured a spot on the *U-615*. During its patrol off the southern Caribbean waters in 1943, the crew complained about the lack of action until they finally destroyed a small Allied tanker. An overjoyed Captain Ralph Kapitzky radioed his success to Berlin, and this served as the ship's downfall. A Puerto Rican tracking station intercepted the captain's message, and on July 29, an American bomber spotted the *U-615* when it surfaced to recharge its batteries. When the plane attacked and caused minor damage, Kapitzky ordered the submarine to crash-dive. Kapitzky guided the vessel toward the Atlantic, where for the next few days, the *U-615* desperately ran and hid to elude sky attacks. Allied planes launched another assault and caused considerable damage. The U-boat crew worked at a feverish pace to repair the vessel. On August 6, 1943, the *U-615* cruised about two hundred miles east of Curaçao, where Kapitzky ordered his crew to surface for repairs. Despite watches, an American bomber caught the crew off guard. The plane dived down on the vessel and bombed the stern. On deck, crew members fired antiaircraft guns and blasted at least one American plane out of the air. Within minutes, another wave of Allied attackers approached and bombed the U-boat. Their deadly strafing left Franke with a painful wound in his shoulder. After dark, the captain ordered that the dead be committed to the sea. The crew awoke the next morning to a battle station's blast. Kapitzky spied an American destroyer, the USS *Walker*, heading directly toward them. Realizing that it was all over, the captain gave the order to abandon ship. He watched until the last of the crew left in lifeboats. Then Kapitzky lowered himself into the hatch and took his vessel to the bottom of the sea. Americans gave the German survivors medical treatment aboard the *Walker*. At Port of Spain, Trinidad, they were issued clean clothing and transported to Norfolk, Virginia. The entire crew staunchly refused to divulge any information other than name, rank and serial number.

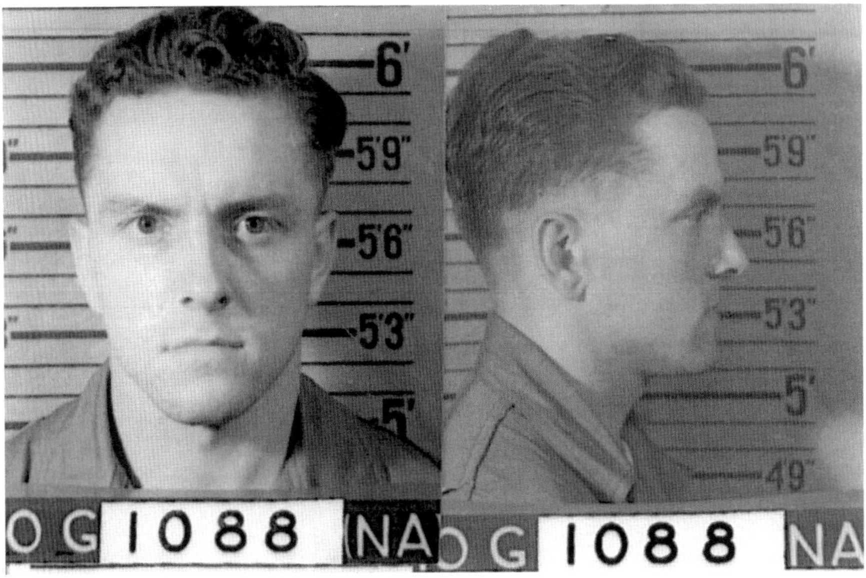

Helmut Fischer, a crew member of the *U-615*, attended a trade school and joined the Hitler Youth group. *Courtesy National Archives, Washington, D.C.*

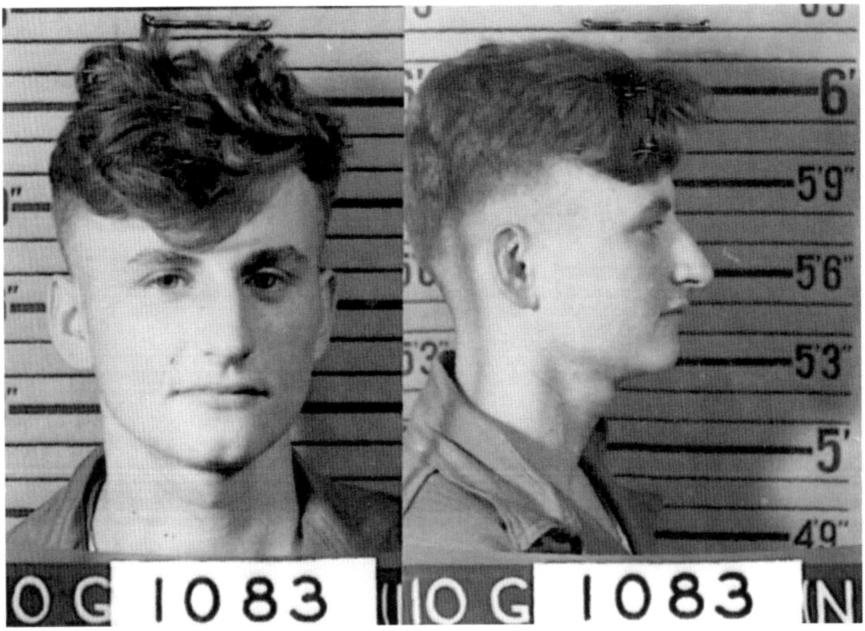

Fritz Franke, a crew member of the *U-615*, was the most resolute Nazi and least cooperative prisoner. *Courtesy National Archives, Washington, D.C.*

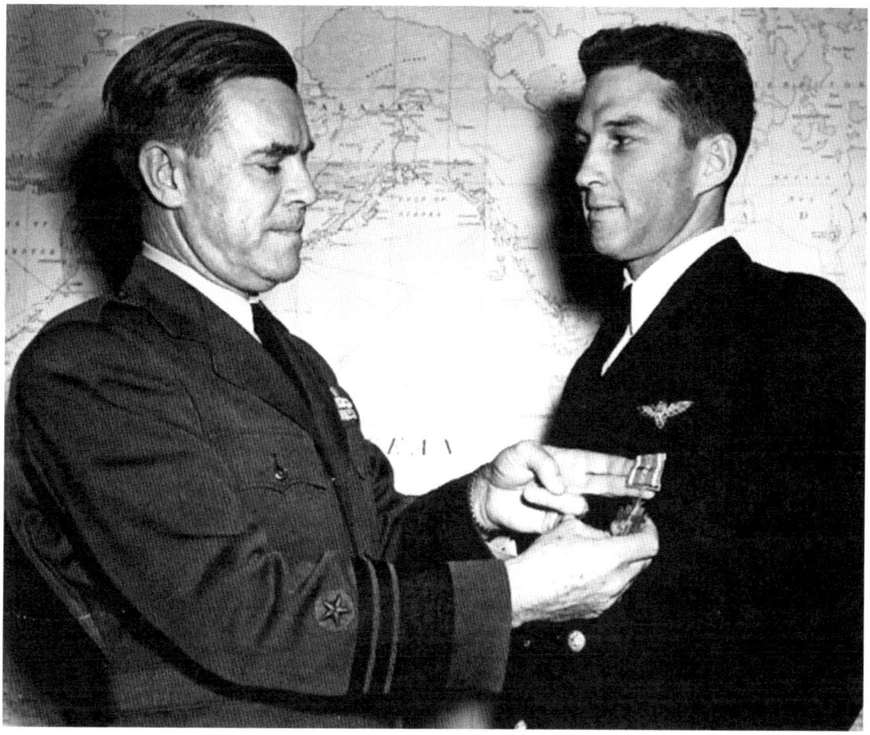

Vice Admiral N.L. Bellinger, commander of the Naval Air Force, Atlantic, presents the Distinguished Flying Cross to Lieutenant Lewis D. Crockett for his part in the sinking of *U-615. Courtesy of Captain Jerry Mason's (Retd.) U-boat Archive.*

The plump Bernhard Reyak was born and raised in the town of Neuss on the banks of the Rhine River. Reyak worked as a metalsmith in Neuss for two years before joining the navy in 1941. He appeared to carry more doubts about Hitler than his colleagues. Rolf Wizuy was both the most unpredictable and most militant in his beliefs.

At Norfolk, they were transferred to the Army Provost Marshal General's Office, and the five men were separated. Kuelsen and Franke were taken to Newport News, Virginia, for interrogation by naval intelligence authorities, and Fischer, Reyak and Wizuy were transported to Fort Meade for more intensive questioning.

The prisoners reunited at Stringtown, Oklahoma, and ultimately at Camp Papago Park, Arizona. Drechsler, born in Chemnitz in East Germany about thirty miles from the Czechoslovakian border, lived in a middle-class home at Number 1 Sebastian Bach Strasse and walked to public school. A good

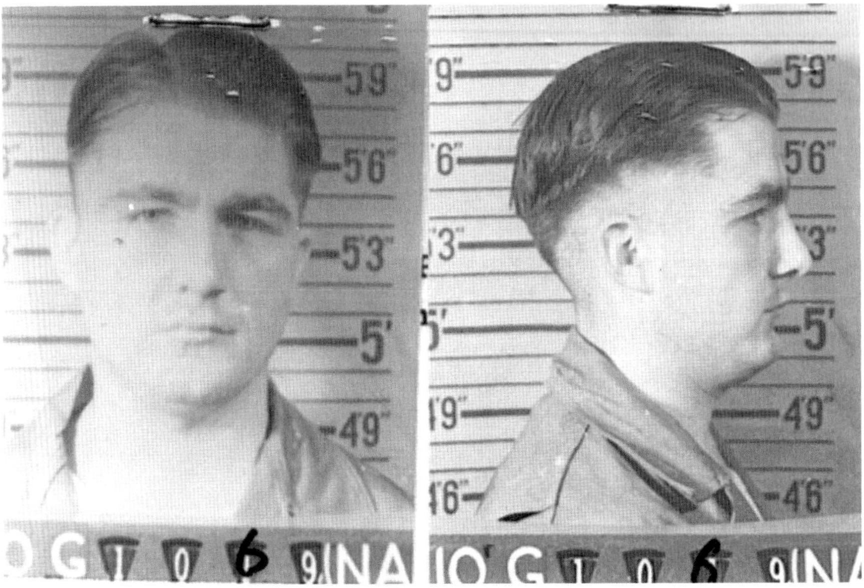

Bernhard Reyak, a member of the *U-615*, appeared to carry more doubts than the others about the execution of Werner Drechsler. *Courtesy National Archives, Washington, D.C.*

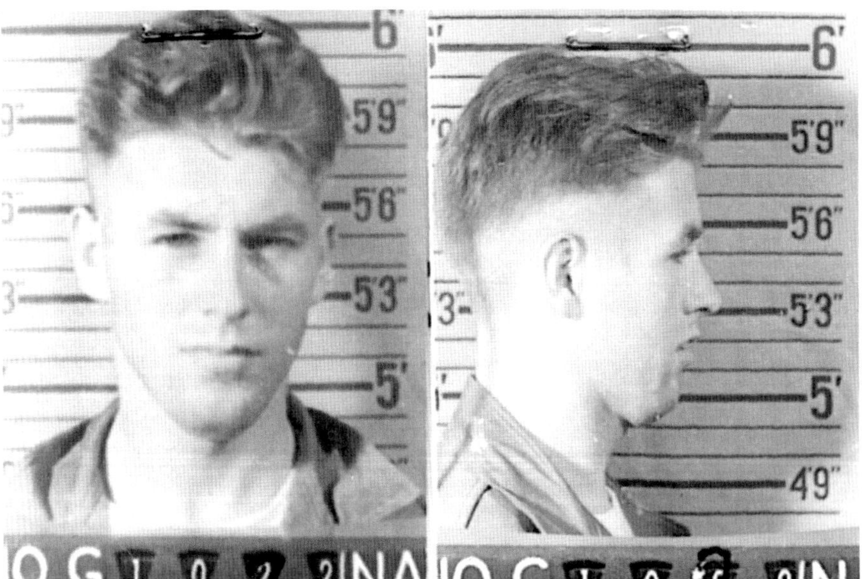

Rolf Wizuy, before joining the *U-615*, worked as an electrician during the day and studied the writings of Hitler, Goebbels and Baldur von Schirach, the virulent leader of the of the Hitler Youth, at night. *Courtesy National Archives, Washington, D.C.*

student with an easy smile and the normal mischief of a young boy, he graduated from the public school system in 1937 just as Hitler began to intrude on the education of German youth. In school, he learned a smattering of French and English, but his real interests were history and the arts. However, Germany was mobilizing for the war, so Drechsler entered a trade school to become a mechanic. He worked for a couple of years in Chemnitz before joining the navy in 1941. He volunteered for U-boat service and was sent to Kiel for advanced submarine training. His first assignment was to the *U-118*, a submarine supply boat and mine layer, sometimes referred to as a "milch cow." On December 8, 1941, the day after Pearl Harbor, the *U-118* was commissioned. The vessel was under the command of Captain Werner Czygan, who was respected by Drechsler and the rest of the crew. The one officer Drechsler and the rest of the crew did not like was Lieutenant Felix Muller, the boat's first engineer. He was referred to disdainfully as "Felix the Strong" because of his bullying tactics and ultimately had to be removed from the boat. The first two war cruises of the *U-118* supplied other subs in the Atlantic. Drechsler was accepted as a good submariner.

One member of the crew was Herman Polowzyk from Poland. He had been drafted into the U-boat service, indicating that Germany was having a

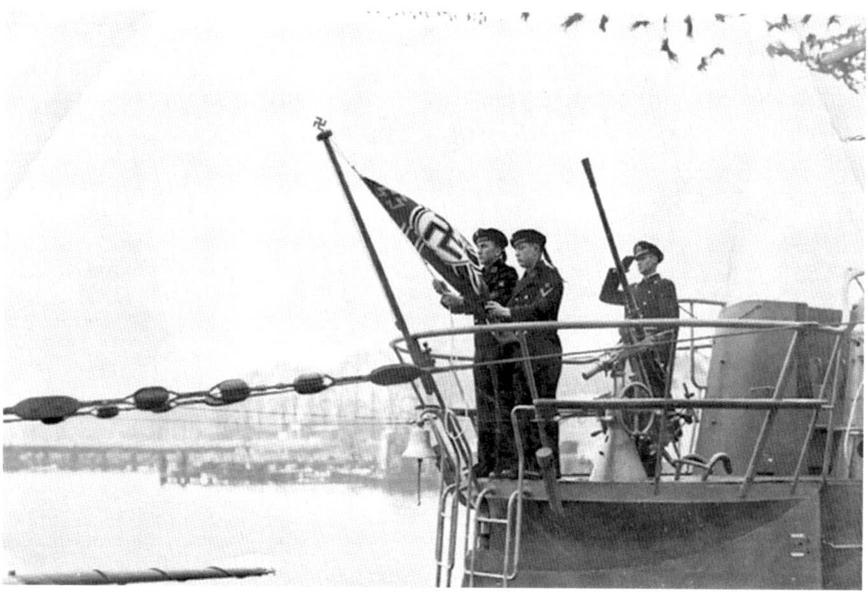

The flag is raised and Drechsler's *U-118* is formally commissioned. *Courtesy National Archives, Washington, D.C.*

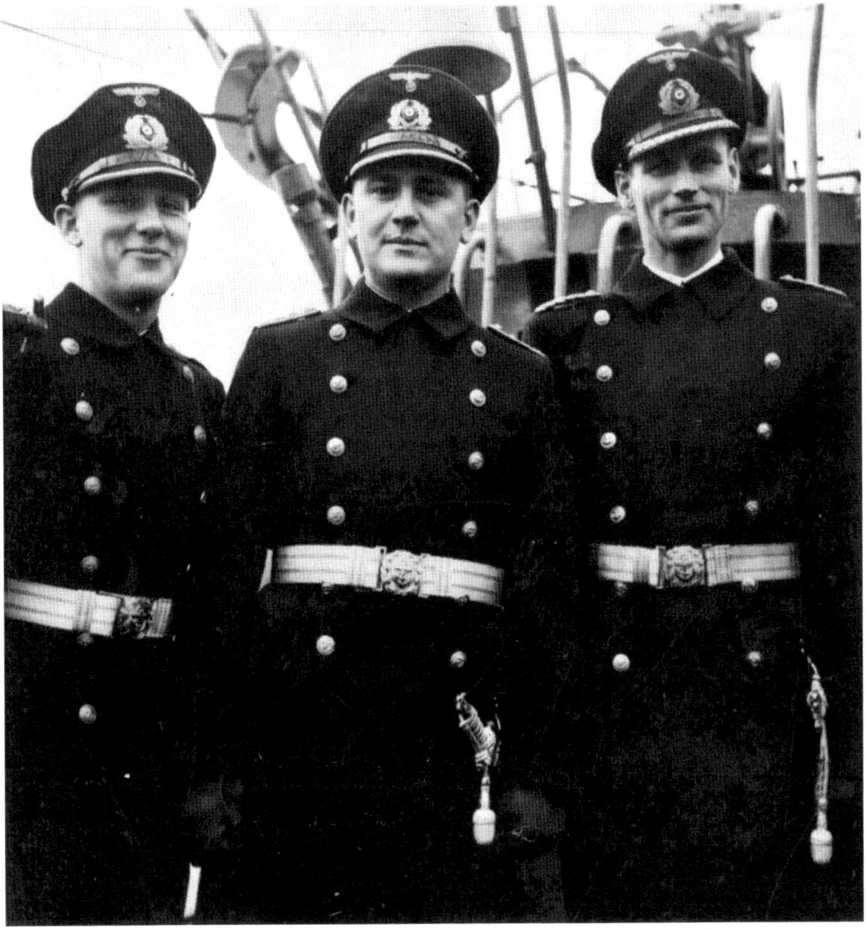

U-118 officers, *left to right*: Watch Officer Lieutenant Falke, Watch Officer Lieutenant Brammer and Captain Werner Czygan. All three men perished in the destruction of the *U-118*. *Courtesy National Archives, Washington, D.C.*

hard time getting qualified crews. Polowzyk, ignored as much as possible in these close quarters, was aware that the crew regarded him as a Pole, not a German. Both Czygan and Drechsler went out of their way to be friendly with him. The captain frequently engaged him in a game of chess in an effort to keep Polowzyk's morale up and to try to be an example to the rest of the crew. Drechsler became friendly with the young Pole, probably because he did not share the Third Reich's racial and nationalistic attitudes and thus did not feel alienated from other races. On the second cruise, the vessel came dangerously close to being crushed in a watery grave but survived when a clogged valve was cleared. It put in to Lorient, France, an Atlantic coastal town, for repairs. On the third cruise, the *U-118* was charged with laying mines in the waters of the Straits of Gibraltar. The fourth and final war cruise of the *U-118* was a mine-laying mission in the Azores.

On June 12, 1943, Drechsler and several crewmen were sunbathing on the deck. Men jumped overboard as the ship was bombarded with torpedoes. Drechsler swam with difficulty and gasped in horror as a plane approached him, but instead of dropping what he supposed would be a bomb, it dropped a life raft. About an hour later, the survivors were picked up by the USS *Osmond Ingram*. Of the fifty-eight-man crew on the *U-118*, only seventeen were alive when the *Osmond Ingram* arrived, but one of the survivors died soon after. Drechsler was taken directly to the ship's sick bay, where his right knee was operated on by the ship's doctor. When he arrived at Norfolk, Virginia, eight days later, he walked with great pain and was helped off the ship by his Polish friend Herman Polowzyk. Drechsler and another wounded prisoner were taken to the naval base hospital while the other fourteen submariners were shipped directly to Fort Meade for interrogation. Drechsler's executioners, Kuelsen and Franke, were removed to Newport News, Virginia, for interrogation, while Fischer, Reyak and Wizuy were sent to Fort Hunt at Alexandria. At Fort Hunt, Wizuy shared a cell with Drechsler, who introduced himself as "Obermaat (Petty Officer) Limmer." Wizuy instinctively distrusted "Limmer" in spite of his friendliness and did not divulge any information of importance. While at Fort Hunt, Wizuy suffered appendicitis. Drechsler solicitously cared for him and brought him ice after his operation. The five *U-615* submariners were reunited at Stringtown, Oklahoma, where they discussed Drechsler's treasonous activities.

American interrogators assessed Drechsler's character as a reliable anti-Nazi but described him as conceited. They based his credibility on his testimony that Hitler had imprisoned his father, a Social Democrat, in a concentration camp for three years. At the time of Drechsler's capture, one brother was serving in the German infantry in Poland and the other served on a minesweeper near Norway. Drechsler demonstrated an aptitude for U-boat service and took advanced submarine training at Kiel. After attending the U-boat school at Gotenhafen and torpedo school at Flensburg, he received an assignment as a torpedo man on the *U-118*.

With a full load of fuel oil, the *U-118* could cruise about twenty thousand nautical miles without refueling. The submarine had left the Germania Werft shipbuilding yard at Kiel on January 6, 1942, for "working up" exercises in the Baltic Sea. Ice trapped the *U-118* and twenty other submarines in Danzig

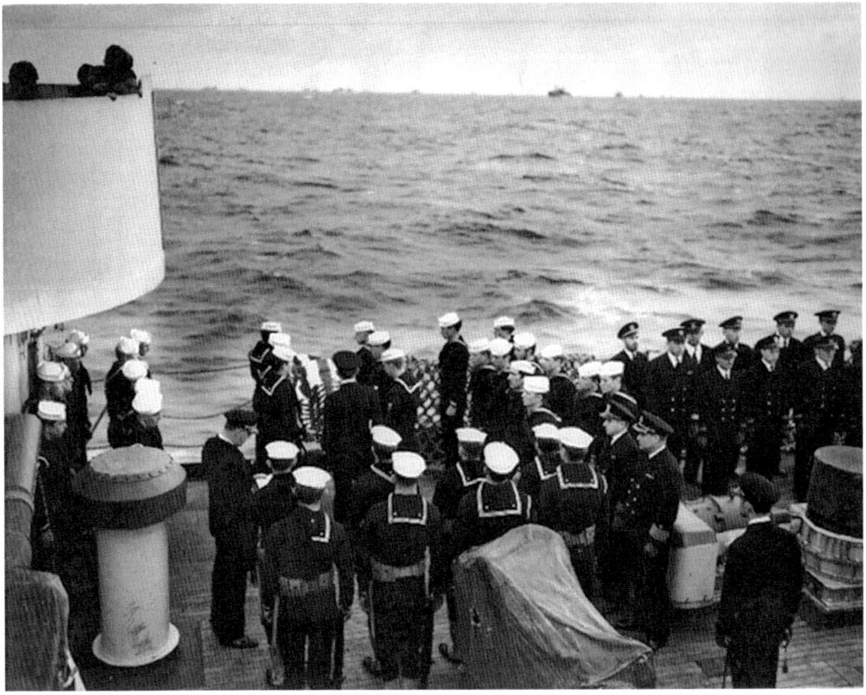

The burial at sea funeral service for Radioman Julius T. Petrella was held at sunset. Harold S. Berdine, commanding officer of *Spencer*, read the ceremony, while the *Spencer*'s crew stood at attention. *Courtesy of Captain Jerry Mason's (Retd.) U-boat Archive.*

from January 8 until March 29. On March 29, the *U-118* pushed slowly through the ice toward Hala. For about one week, several U-boats practiced firing torpedoes northeast of the Hala peninsula. During its second mission from April 26 to May 4, it scouted the waters near Bornholm, a Danish island in the Baltic Sea. From May 12 to 14, it successfully laid mines in the Skagerrak Sea on the northern tip of Denmark. During its third mission in February 1943, the *U-118* laid mines in the hazardous Straits of Gibraltar near Tangier. Drechsler said that many of the crew put on their identification tags before they left because they had to be ready for anything, as this floating powder keg was very near the well-fortified English base of Gibraltar.

After all the mines were placed, the submarine headed toward the Atlantic. Several times it dived when it spotted Allied aircraft. The *U-118* came dangerously close to being crushed in a watery grave on December 7, when it submerged after supplying another U-boat. The crew could not stop the submarine's descent. When the *U-118* finally righted itself, someone discovered that a valve had become clogged with debris that had been tossed overboard during the last supply transfer. The engineer, Felix Muller, lost his head and cried, "What shall I do?" Czygan ordered him to blow the tanks. Mueller complied but forgot to close one diving tank, making the situation even more precarious. The *U-118* shot steeply upward out of the water, and finally the forward part of the vessel slapped violently down on the water's surface. Drechsler said that every man had given up hope of survival during this crisis. The next day, the crew celebrated the *U-118*'s first anniversary as well as their deliverance from a watery grave. The captain provided an extra good meal with cake, and each man toasted the crew's good fortune with a bottle of beer. Czygan guided the vessel, which had considerable damage, into Bordeaux, France, where he had the valve repaired and the engine overhauled. During this two-month period, the *U-118* crew members traveled in groups of six to the naval antiaircraft school near Biaritz for a five-day submarine flak course. While at Bordeaux, the crew received news from an incoming submarine that it had successfully laid mines along the American coast.

Drechsler told his interrogators that Bordeaux harbored many Nazi sympathizers and German U-boats often put in here for repairs. While in Bordeaux, Drechsler learned that *U-118* mines had damaged three British vessels—the *Mary Slessor*, the *Empire Mordred* and the *Baltonia*—and sank the Spanish *Duero*. Drechsler said that the Germans were quartered in barracks named after German towns and districts, and every night a bus transported the Germans to the brothels. He bragged about being invited to dine with members of the French aristocracy. Drechsler's vessel left Bordeaux for its fourth and final patrol on May 22, 1943, carrying a full load of sixty-six mines. The crew frequently tuned into U.S. news and music broadcasts but became disgusted with the amount of advertising.

The final attack on the *U-118* is described in terse military language from memories of the surviving POWs. Immediately upon sighting the *U-118*, Lieutenant R.L. Stearns signaled Lieutenant R.F. Johnson for the USS *Bogue* to deploy planes and make a strafing run. The *Bogue* joined the Atlantic Fleet in February 1943 as the nucleus of the anti-submarine hunter-killer group. Aircraft operating from the *Bogue* sank eleven German and two Japanese submarines, making it the most successful anti-submarine carrier in World War II. Johnson dove directly at the *U-118* stern and strafed from three thousand feet on down to about fifteen feet above the water, going over the U-boat from stern to bow. Stearns attacked the *U-118* after Johnson finished the first run. When one hundred feet over water, Stearns released bombs in pairs that straddled the U-boat amidships. The U-boat made a dive at the explosion of depth charges. It resurfaced at a very slow speed. At this time, the U-boat's decks were awash. It traveled for about seventy-five yards before sinking to about twenty-five feet, trailing oil and air bubbles. Lieutenants W.S. Fowler and Tennant arrived. Fowler attacked the U-boat when it resurfaced the second time. Tennant strafed it twice and then circled and strafed only when men in the conning tower tried to man the guns. Finally, Fowler got on one side and Tennant the other, and they chased the men back and forth across the deck. The crew didn't jump overboard but donned life jackets. When Lieutenant Fryatt arrived on scene, the U-boat listed to starboard and sank slowly. Fryatt started to make another run to drop his remaining depth charges, but by the time he got into position to drop again, people were jumping overboard and the *U-118*'s stern was so low in the water that he didn't think it necessary to drop the depth charges. When Lieutenants W.F. Chamberlain and R.S. Rogers arrived, they saw smoke or spray rising from the U-boat. Rogers made one run, and then Chamberlain dove to attack, dropping two depth charges that exploded directly under the U-boat's conning tower. During this run, the *U-118* got off a few bursts of fire. Chamberlain dropped the remaining two depth charges, which also exploded directly under the U-boat. The boat blew up, sending large pieces of metal and debris high in the air.

All officers on board the *U-118* were killed in the conning tower at the time of the attack, four dead men were left in the water and seventeen men were picked up by the *Osmond Ingram*. Drechsler recalled seeing Czygan on one knee on deck with blood spurting out of his white shirt.

The *U-118* carried sixty days' of provisions in large tin containers, including meat, vegetables, fruit and eighty-five thousand cigarettes. Werner Reinl, who would later testify against Drechsler, helped three injured comrades descend into the hatch. Czygan gave the order to submerge. When the U-boat dropped to a depth of thirty-five meters, the first charges hit and exploded near the stern, causing considerable damage. When water poured into the diesel compartment, the crew switched on the emergency system. After several more depth charges struck, the U-boat's motors went dead, the electrical steering failed and the rudder came loose. The vessel sank to fifty-five meters. Josef Grosz wept when he could no longer keep the vessel afloat. Czygan gave an order to resurface and fight it out with the planes. The astonished gunnery crew saw eight planes diving toward them. Heavy strafing cut down gunnery submariners in their tracks.

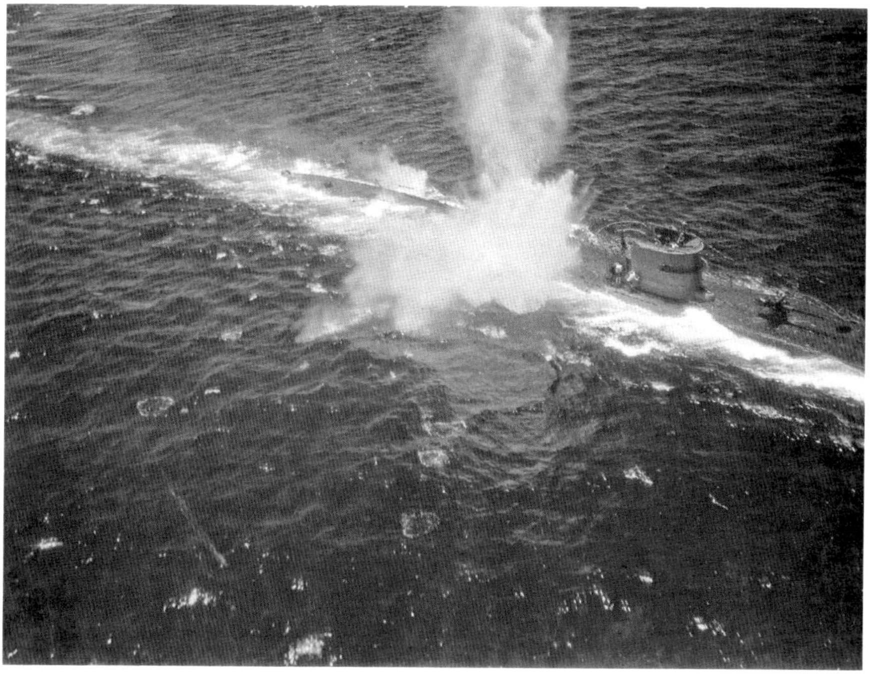

Drechsler's U-boat, the *U-118*, under attack on June 12, 1943. *Courtesy of Captain Jerry Mason's (Retd.) U-boat Archive.*

Drechsler worked below decks until a motor exploded and burst into flames. A machinist burned to death, and Drechsler climbed on deck. After receiving another depth charge, the *U-118* split in half and sank. A fragment ripped Drechsler's neck open, and a bullet hit him in the knee. Czygan gave the order to abandon the ship and gave the first emergency signal indicating the latitude and longitude of the boat; a few seconds later, he signaled, "Boat is sinking." Finally, Czygan gave the code name of the boat. The submarine carried only one rubber lifeboat. Drechsler plunged into the water. Czygan remained on the bridge throughout the attack. Czygan, age thirty-eight, left a wife and a daughter.

About an hour later, the *U-118* survivors, including Drechsler, were picked up by the USS *Osmond Ingram*. Of the fifty-seven-man crew, only seventeen survived. One survivor died a few minutes after his rescue. His shipmates stood by him during the ceremony when his body was committed to the sea. Drechsler was taken directly to the sick bay, where the ship's doctor operated on his right knee and removed a bullet. When he arrived at Norfolk, Virginia, eight days later, Drechsler limped with great pain, and Herman

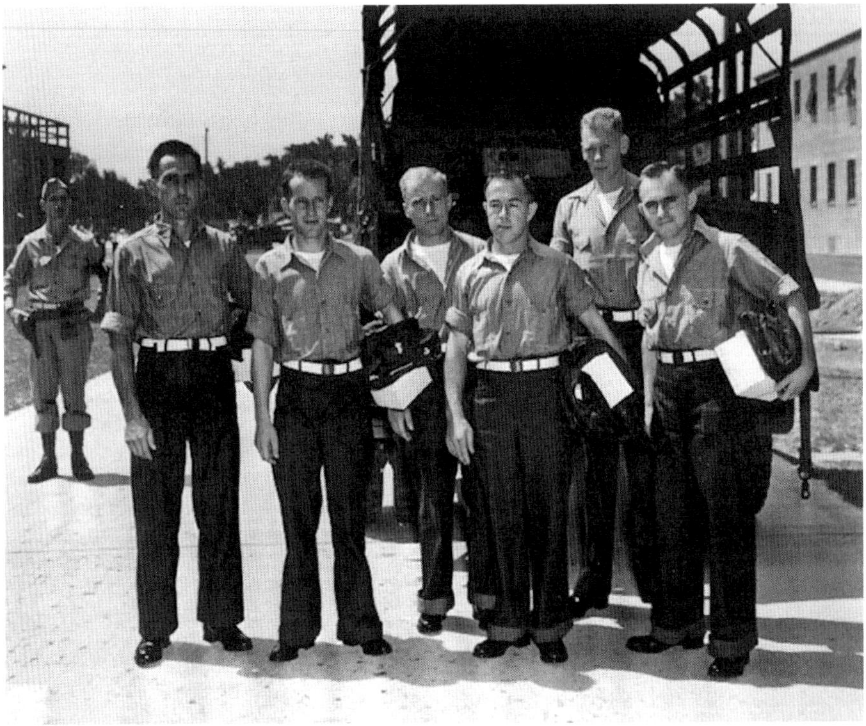

Senior *U-118* survivors after their physical examinations and initial POW processing. *Left to right:* Josef Grosz, Josef Holler, Rudolf Wiemer, Werner Reinl, Hans Siebert and Hermann Wiedemann. *Courtesy of Captain Jerry Mason's (Retd.) U-boat Archive.*

Polowzyk helped him off the ship. Wounded prisoners, including Drechsler, were immediately removed to the naval base hospital. The uninjured *U-118* submariners were shipped to Fort Hunt.

After nine days in the hospital, the navy transferred Drechsler to Fort Hunt. By the time he arrived, several of his crew mates had already been transferred to Stringtown, Oklahoma. Others remained at Fort Hunt for intervals of a single day to several weeks, depending on their level of cooperation and on the amount and type of information they gave the authorities. Drechsler remained at Fort Hunt for seven months. He proved to be not only anti-Nazi but also very cooperative. The Office of Naval Intelligence determined that part of his value as a prisoner might be to win the confidence and extract information from other German prisoners. The Americans assigned Drechsler to bugged rooms with German prisoners. He passed on the information gleaned from these conversations to American naval authorities. Although he extracted some information, most of the

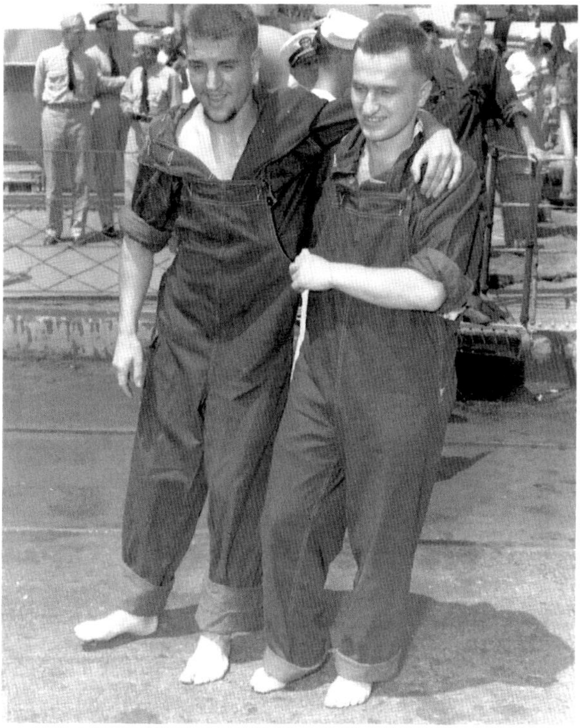

Werner Drechsler, recovering from a bullet wound to his right knee, disembarks USS *Osmond Ingram* assisted by Herman Polowzyk. *Courtesy of Captain Jerry Mason's (Retd.) U-boat Archive.*

German prisoners did not trust him and said nothing. Drechsler provided the Americans with detailed drawings of the *U-118* and its day-to-day operations. He described a camp in his hometown of Chemnitz where American, British, French and Russian soldiers were being held prisoner. He drew a map of Chemnitz, showing strategic railroad and government sites. He also provided information on the German U-boat radio school at Le Touquet, France.

During this period, Drechsler improved his English. One interrogation officer insisted, "Drechsler is so cooperative that he should never be sent to a camp where other German Navy prisoners are interned." At Stringtown, Oklahoma, the prisoners talked about Drechsler, whom many knew as "Limmer," "Leimi" and "Nimmer." Here, Rolf Wizuy met Heinrich Ludwig. They reviewed their experiences at Fort Hunt and discussed how a so-called U-boatman had tried to get military information from them. Before long, they realized that they were talking about the same man but with different names. Wizuy knew Drechsler as "Leimi" and as an officer. Ludwig said the man told him his name was "Limmer" and claimed that he had served on the *U-118*. Two men from the *U-118* had not been accounted for, and one of the descriptions fit Drechsler. Wizuy and Ludwig discovered that several German officers and at least fifteen ordinary seamen gave strikingly similar descriptions of a German who attempted to question them.

All POWs were immediately interrogated upon arriving in the United States. Friedrich Murza was captured with the sinking of the *U-487* while on its second patrol by planes from the aircraft carrier USS *Core*. Its commander, Helmut Metz, was killed in the action. Of the fifty-eight-man crew, three officers and thirty men were rescued by the USS *Barker*, but two of the men died of their wounds before reaching land and were buried at sea. Seventeen others needed immediate medical attention for machine gun wounds, burns and internal injuries caused by depth charge explosions. The doctor aboard the *Tarazed* had to amputate the arm of one of the men. Seventeen wounded men were hospitalized, and the remainder were transferred to an interrogation center. During Murza's initial interrogation, he was described as thoroughly reliable with good radio knowledge and a likeable chap who was not security conscious. He was sick of the war and wished the damn thing was over. Murza knew Drechsler as Limmer at Fort Hunt, and on August 9, 1943, the U.S. Navy monitored a discussion between Murza and Drechsler. For a while they laughed and talked about food and drink. Then Drechsler tried unsuccessfully to engage Murza in a conversation about munitions and the size of Murza's U-boat.

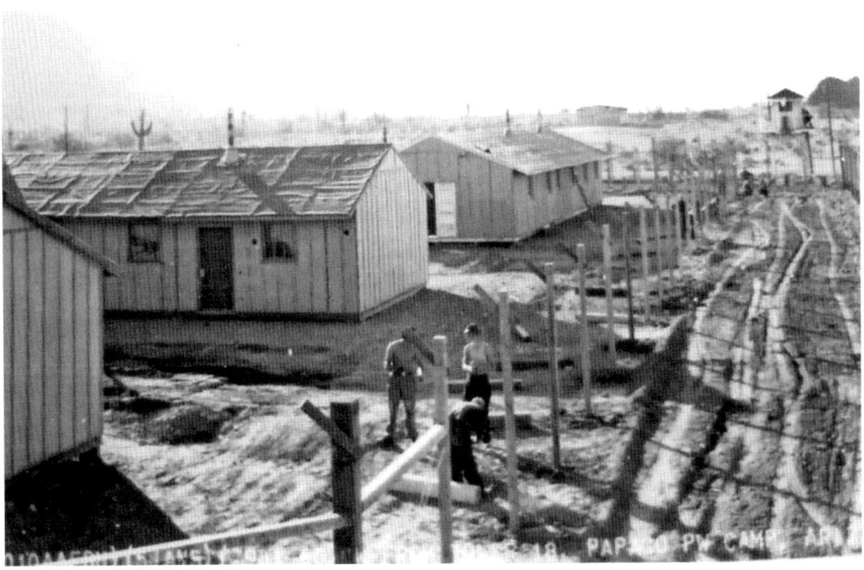

Camp Papago Park, Arizona, was originally built by POWs. *Courtesy Dorothy and Lawrence Jorgensen.*

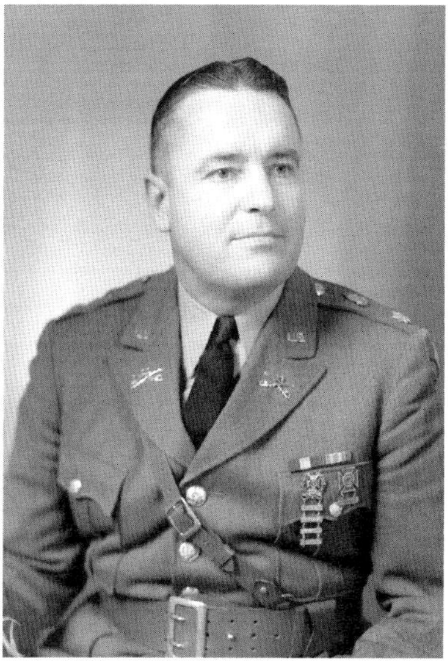

Colonel Verne Austin, a native Arizonan, took over Papago Park from William Holden and managed the dismantling of Camp Papago Park. *Courtesy National Archives, Washington, D.C.*

The German submariners assumed that Stringtown would be their permanent camp until after the war. Then in January 1944, a military order came down transferring all U-boat prisoners to Camp Papago Park, Arizona. With patriotic zeal at an all-time feverish pitch on both sides, dealing with the enemy constituted treason. A prisoner's worst fate was to be labeled a snitch, and prisoners took advantage of every opportunity to proclaim their loyalty to Hitler. On February 7, 1945, they hung a homemade banner with a black swastika from the back of their transportation truck. A group of citizens, including a banker, the town marshal, a deputy sheriff and several businessmen, gave chase, stopped the truck and demanded that the flag be turned over to them. Captain George Childress informed the citizens that they had no business stopping a government vehicle. Moreover, if they took any further action, he would place them under arrest. The banker reported the matter to Colonel John Matten at Camp Papago Park, who told him in no uncertain terms to mind his own business.[22] The new Camp Papago Park commander, Colonel Verne Austin, smoothed over matters between the military and townsfolk, but not before the offended banker wrote a letter to Congressman Richard Harless stating that the Senate should initiate an investigation into military camp practices. From that time, prisoner crews were routed around the large population centers.

The crew from Drechsler's boat occupied the same barracks, but Fischer, Franke, Kuelsen, Reyak and Wizuy bunked in a different barracks. Noncommissioned officers lodged in their own barracks. A typical day at Camp Papago Park began with reveille at 5:30 a.m., breakfast at 6:00 a.m. and work at 7:30 a.m. If the men chose to work in the fields, lunch was provided; otherwise, they marched back to their quarters. All prisoners were supposed to be back in their compound by 5:00 p.m. During the evenings and on Sundays, they suffered from intense homesickness and loneliness.

They wrote letters and talked of escape, home and friends. POWs eagerly awaited the arrival of newcomers for news from home and the war.

On March 3, 1944, the Department of War—with General William Shedd, commander of the U.S. Army's Ninth Service Command, Fort Douglas, Utah; and General Paul B. Clemens, director of Security and Intelligence Division—designated Camp Papago Park, Arizona, as the camp to house all German naval prisoners.[23] German submariners poured into Camp Papago Park. Early arrivals earned money by working on new buildings. While serving as a prisoner of war camp, Camp Papago Park had four commanding officers: Colonel Allen H. Means, September 16, 1943–mid-March 1944; Colonel George Barber, March 1944–August 1, 1944; Colonel William Holden, August 1, 1944–February 11, 1945; and Colonel Verne Austin, February 11, 1945–April 8, 1946. Means activated Camp Papago Park as a prisoner of war camp on September 16, 1943, and took custody of the first large group of Germans on January 5, 1944. Means, who had served in World War I, was a geologist before the war and afterward worked as an administrator for the Wisconsin State Penal System. He received a reputation for permissiveness and was replaced with Colonel George Barber. Barber instituted stringent administrative control measures. He insisted on crossover roll calls even on Sunday mornings and prescribed a maintenance guide for the facilities right down to the cleaning of the latrines. Most of the staff resented Barber, who appeared to do very little work, but his Prussian bearing made him respected among the Germans. He enjoyed swimming in the canals and horseback riding. He visited frequently with Wattenberg, ostensibly to obtain information. On a hot August

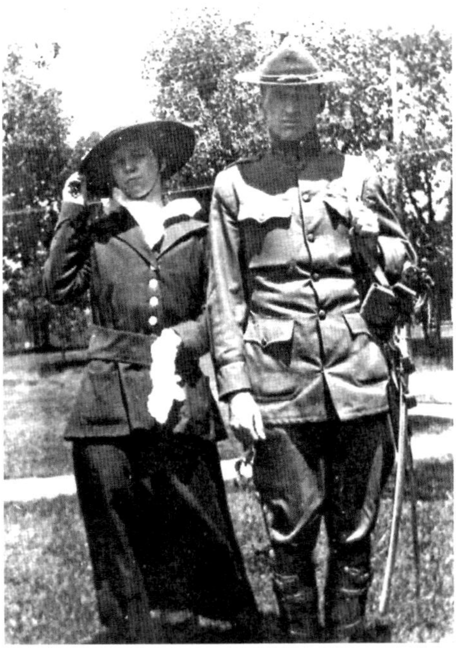

Colonel William A. Holden with his wife, Ruby. Holden, a World War I veteran, had extensive experience in operating prisoner of war camps. *Courtesy Sparta Wisconsin Historical Society.*

morning, Barber turned over the post to Colonel William A. Holden, a World War I veteran who had extensive experience in setting up prisoner of war camps. Holden was one of the most professional of the camp commanders. He tried to keep those with strong Nazi beliefs separate from the others. Holden was a soldier's soldier, a thin-faced man from Sparta, Wisconsin, who had earned a Silver Star and Purple Heart while an infantryman in France during World War I. He had empathy for the soldiers who shouldered the real burdens of war. Performers in the camp's orchestra and theater ensemble so impressed Holden that he paid them for their practice time and performances, in violation of army regulations. However, he suffered from a severe heart problem and was too ill to attend the court-martial of Drechsler's executioners. He discontinued the practice of roll call on Sundays and holidays. Colonel Verne Austin, a native Arizonan, took over from Holden on February 11, 1945, and managed the dismantling of Camp Papago Park. Austin's graduate studies in geology at the University of Nebraska had been interrupted by World War I.[24] He was a career military officer and received many medals, including the Legion of Merit.

Camp Papago Park received good inspection reports, except for prisoner clothing, during its first full month of operation from both the United States military and the Swiss legation, which acted as a protecting power for Germany. Prisoners at Camp Papago Park received a short military haircut and were issued pants and shirts stenciled with six-inch letters "PW." Inspectors criticized the prisoners' practice of running around in their shorts during the summer with no upper garment. All prisoners received ten cents per day in canteen scrip, with which they could purchase toiletries and cigarettes. Officers exercised their right to refuse to work and threatened their subordinates who did work. Trustworthy enlisted Germans could volunteer for work and earn an additional eighty cents a day in the mess halls, laundries and motor pools. They also picked cotton; harvested potatoes, onions, melons and grapes; baled hay; and cleaned irrigation ditches.

CHAPTER 3
SUNDAY IN THE PARK

POWs tried to bring some normalcy to their lives. Friedrich Murza built miniature battleships. Hellmut Rathke painted watercolors. Helmut Micha, a crewman on the *U-513*, maintained a menagerie of seventeen doves, eleven rabbits, twenty-four chickens, five ducks and an Irish setter. The POWs formed Orchestra Camp Papago, and one of their favorite songs was "Don't Fence Me In."[25] However, barbed wire, guard towers and Nazi officers such as Captain Jurgen Wattenberg kept them aware that their lives were anything but normal. The Germans feared Wattenberg, who considered the slightest cooperation with Americans high treason. Americans designated Wattenberg, who died on November 28, 1995, at age ninety-four, as a super-Nazi. After graduation in 1921 from the Naval Academy at Ploen, he joined the navy. As the navigation officer on the pocket battleship *Graf Spee*, he had ordered the scuttling of the damaged vessel outside the harbor of Montevideo, Uruguay, in December 1939. Wattenberg was brought to Buenos Aires on December 18, 1939, for internment. The officers were required to give their word of honor not to leave the city without written permission from the police authorities. The German Embassy attempted to have the *Graf Spee* survivors declared "shipwrecked" to avoid internment, but the fact that the Germans had made arrangements for vessels to pick up survivors before *Graf Spee* sailed for the last time caused the Argentine government to insist on internment. By March 16, 1940, thirty-one officers, including Wattenberg, had escaped with forged passports provided by the German Embassy. The exact route taken to Peru by Wattenberg is not known, but planes, buses and horses crossing the Andes were used by various other prisoners.

At Callao, Peru, he embarked on a Japanese steamer for Germany, and before long he was given command of the *U-162.* Wattenberg spoke on the German radio on June 20, 1942, broadcasting his successes. He claimed the sinking of nine ships and described the sinking of the Brazilian *Parmahyba* as "presenting a spectacle of singular beauty." The *U-162* was sunk by the schooner *Florence M. Douglas* on September 3, 1942. Forty-nine survived from the crew of fifty-one. Wattenberg had made a fatal blunder. His single torpedo broke the surface and betrayed his position, sealing the fate of his boat. The explosion of depth charges in the first attack caused a leak in the *U-162*. Water entered the boat, and it went down. Prisoners told the story of three pigs that survived the sinking of *U-162*. One pig was kept in the engine room for the duration of the second cruise, and the other was eaten.

Wattenberg, along with others, was captured and taken to Fort Meade and then to Crossville, Tennessee. On January 27, 1944, Wattenberg, along with seventy-nine officers and twenty-seven enlisted men, boarded the train at Crossville and headed for Camp Papago Park. Dorothy Jorgensen processed Wattenberg when he arrived at Camp Papago Park. He informed her that he had been promoted to a full captain and as such would not consent to be processed until she addressed him with his new ranking. Moreover, he would refuse to submit to a roll call by any American whose rank was not equal to his own. Prisoners, behind Wattenberg's back, encouraged Jorgensen to refuse his demands. She won the dispute.[26] Wattenberg masterminded the *faustball* tunnel and instigated the murder of Werner Drechsler. However, after the war, he participated in the Papago Trackers organization and frequently visited Arizona. In his later years, when he could no longer attend events, he sent regards to the organization.

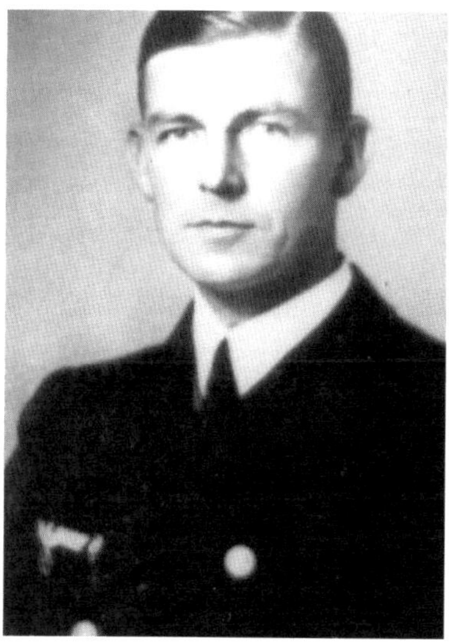

Camp Papago Park prisoners came under the control of the ranking Nazi officer, Captain Jurgen Wattenberg. *Courtesy National Archives, Washington, D.C.*

Arizonans were unhappy with the Germans who refused to work, and while work was voluntary, a diet of bread and

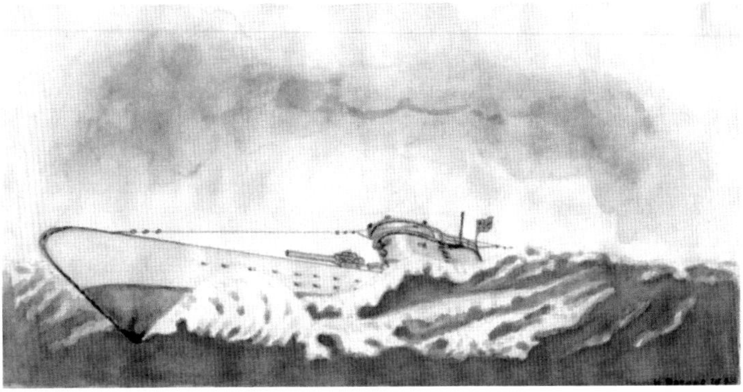

While at Camp Papago Park, Hellmut Rathke did a watercolor of the *U-352*. *Courtesy of Captain Jerry Mason's (Retd.) U-boat Archive.*

water ensured a large farm labor pool. Prisoners could not be forced to work in any industry directly related to the war effort, and Wattenberg insisted that Arizona cotton was vital to America's war effort and accused subordinates who worked in the cotton fields of treason. Arizonans were unhappy with the Germans who refused to work. The Swiss legation supported the Americans, citing Geneva Convention Article 27, which stipulated that "belligerents may utilize the labor of able prisoners of war." When Wattenberg's attitude became increasingly belligerent, Barber segregated him from all other prisoners in the camp. Other serious troublemakers were transferred to Camp Alva, Oklahoma. The Ninth Service Command considered Wattenberg's transfer to another camp unwise in that it would be expensive with no material benefits. Two officers, Eugene Richter and Horst von Pflugk-Harttung, were transferred to Camp Papago Park to try to control Wattenberg.[27]

Pflugk-Harttung was violently opposed to all things Socialistic, Communistic and Asiatic. He had been accused of having engineered the murders of Rosa Luxemburg and Karl Liebknecht, founders of the German Communist Party. Wattenberg retained control of the camp, and nothing stifled his Nazi activities.

On any given day, Camp Papago Park officials experienced routine discipline problems: missed roll call, stealing an American officer's uniform, creating a disturbance, disobeying an American officer, concocting an intoxicating liquor by mixing beer and fermented fruit juices and devising various methods of escape. These misconducts were accepted, but not the forbidden Heil Hitler salute and goose-stepping. Punishment usually consisted of a couple days in the guardhouse with subsistence on bread and water. The good reports that Camp Papago Park had first received stopped, and the camp became less well regulated.

Several prisoners escaped more than once from Camp Papago Park, and the commanders spent much of their time explaining to their superiors why the camp was in such disorder. When asked to furnish photographs of the escapees, Means admitted that he had none. To tighten up security, Means recommended fingerprinting, issuing "V"-heeled shoes, taking photographs and improving communication with civilian law enforcement agents. On August 1, 1944, Shedd replaced Means with Colonel William Holden, who served as the commander during the *faustball* tunnel exodus and during Drechsler's murder. His inspection revealed that the camp walls had little or no insulation and roofs leaked. Gypsum board covered most of the enlisted men's quarters, but in places it had been replaced with paper. The stockade's main gates were partially buried in mud and could not be used. The sentry made no attempt to identify either incoming or outgoing people or vehicles. Because the keys to the gates of Compounds 1 and 2 could not be found, the gates simply remained open all the time.

In other ways, Camp Papago Park had much to recommend it. The infirmary provided excellent medical care. Two American army doctors and nine German doctors attended to both the American personnel and the German prisoners. Three American dentists and one German dentist took care of the dental problems. Prisoners could attend either Catholic or Lutheran church services, but church attendance was low because the Nazis felt that those in need of spiritual aid were weak. The Camp Papago Park Library contained 1,600 German novels, 600 nonfiction German books, 400 English novels and 350 English educational books that had been brought from Stringtown, Oklahoma, or donated by the German Red Cross. Several prisoners had brought their musical instruments from Stringtown, and before long, Orchestra Camp Papago provided entertainment. German officers conducted classes under the auspices of the University of Minnesota. Lieutenant Helmut Schulze taught English. Other courses included French, Spanish, history, geography and mathematics.

While Werner Drechsler was the only prisoner of war to be murdered at Camp Papago Park, he was not the only one to suffer physical abuse and psychological threats by fanatical Nazis. Hermann Ritter, a Czech, informed on Jurgen Wattenberg when the captain encouraged sabotage and ordered the prisoners to make as much trouble as possible. After Wattenberg found out about this, the Nazis threatened Ritter, who was taken into protective custody. Barber recommended that he be transferred to an anti-Nazi camp.[28] Five officers petitioned Holden for protective custody and a transfer out of Camp Papago Park. These prisoners lived in fear of their lives after Wattenberg threatened them for requesting suitable work. His compatriots brutally beat Otto Handling after he was tried and convicted in a mock court at Camp Papago Park for appropriating canteen checks belonging to other prisoners of war. Captain Hellmut Rathke, from the *U-362*, supplanted Wattenberg for a brief period as camp spokesman, but it was not in Wattenberg's nature to remain in the background. Before long, the two men were fighting, and Wattenberg, along with other officers, accused Rathke of being anti-Nazi. To get out of the compound and into a hospital, Rathke waged a hunger strike.

On February 4, 1944, seven months after Drechsler's arrival in the United States, the navy decided that they had obtained all of his worthwhile information and he would go to Camp Papago Park, without consideration of his special status. For Camp Papago Park prisoners Helmut Fischer, Fritz Franke, Guenther Kuelsen, Heinrich Ludwig, Bernhard Reyak, Rolf Wizuy and Otto Stengel, March 12, 1944, would be a pivotal day in their young lives. At 5:30 a.m., the whistle blasted them out of bed. Once outside, they fell into their assigned formation for roll call in front of the barracks. Sundays were leisurely at Camp Papago Park. Prisoners might be on duty in the mess halls or perform odd jobs around the camp. However, most of the men would be free to attend church services, see a movie, play soccer or write letters. The movie always drew a large afternoon crowd even though it featured a censored American propaganda film.

Drechsler had celebrated his twenty-first birthday without ceremony two months earlier at Fort Hunt. Stocky and athletic, with wounds in his neck and leg that frequently became infected, he also suffered from tuberculosis. Before transferring to Camp Papago Park, Drechsler had been transferred to Fort Leonard Wood, Missouri, where he was treated for tuberculosis and kept away from other prisoners as much as possible. In the early morning hours of March 12, 1944, Drechsler boarded a train headed for Camp Papago Park, Arizona, where he arrived at about 3:00 p.m. that afternoon. POWs questioned the newcomers, anxious to learn something of the war outside the prison walls. Drechsler started off by bragging about how good the Americans had been to him and how Germany would lose the war. It was not an auspicious introduction, and within an hour, the prisoners were suspicious that a traitor had arrived in their midst. Noncommissioned officers maintained communication with their officers and enlisted men in spite of efforts by the Americans to enforce segregation. Their methods included throwing bottles containing messages over the fences, sending notices via mirror signals and hiding memorandums under rocks. Reyak succeeded in contacting Chief Quartermaster Franz Hox and asked him to get a message regarding Drechsler's presence to Wattenberg. Drechsler's crew mates insisted that any action against him should be carried out either by those who had personal knowledge of his treason or by those selected by German officers. That evening, most of the prisoners, haunted by Wattenberg's inflamed exhortations to rid the camp of non-Nazis, thought about Drechsler. Two tower searchlights regularly scanned the grounds, and in the distance, the Germans could see the inviting city lights of Phoenix. The camp was enclosed by two rows of barbed wire, ten feet apart.

After Rolf Wizuy made a positive identification of Drechsler, they discussed what should be done with him. Several POWs speculated that the worst punishment they could safely get away with would be the "Holy Ghost" or *Heilige Geist*. During the Holy Ghost, the assailants would sneak up on their prey, toss a blanket or coat over his head and then beat him mercilessly. They were careful to make no vocal sounds so the victim never saw or heard his attackers and could not identify them.

After the thrashing, they would ostracize Drechsler for the duration of the war. They believed that after Germany won the war, he would get his just punishment. Wizuy and others insisted that the only just punishment for Drechsler was immediate death. Guenther Bleise was only nineteen when his boat, the *U-513*, was destroyed on July 19, 1943, and survivors were taken to Brazil. Bleise ordered Wizuy, Fischer, Kuelsen, Franke, Ludwig and Reyak to report to Hox, who sat at a table in the orderly room of Compound 4 and held a "kangaroo court." Outside, prisoners stood guard on lookout for American patrols. Besides the seven prisoners implicated in Drechsler's murder, Friedrich Murza, Siegfried Elser, Otto Stengel, Werner Reinl and several noncommissioned officers attended this meeting.

Hox listened intently as Wizuy and his comrades told their stories regarding Drechsler's treachery. When Heinrich Ludwig received word from Bleise to report to Hox, he put on a clean shirt and dashed out the door. For Ludwig, the moment had arrived when he, too, must identify Drechsler as a traitor.

From inside the barracks, he heard Hox say, "Well, it appears clear to me now. It is Drechsler."

An unidentified voice inquired, "What should we do about him?"

Hox ignored the question and asked Ludwig to present his account. Ludwig told how he had roomed with Drechsler for about ten days in an interrogation camp near Washington, D.C. He knew their conversations had been repeated to Americans because the authorities questioned him about specifics.

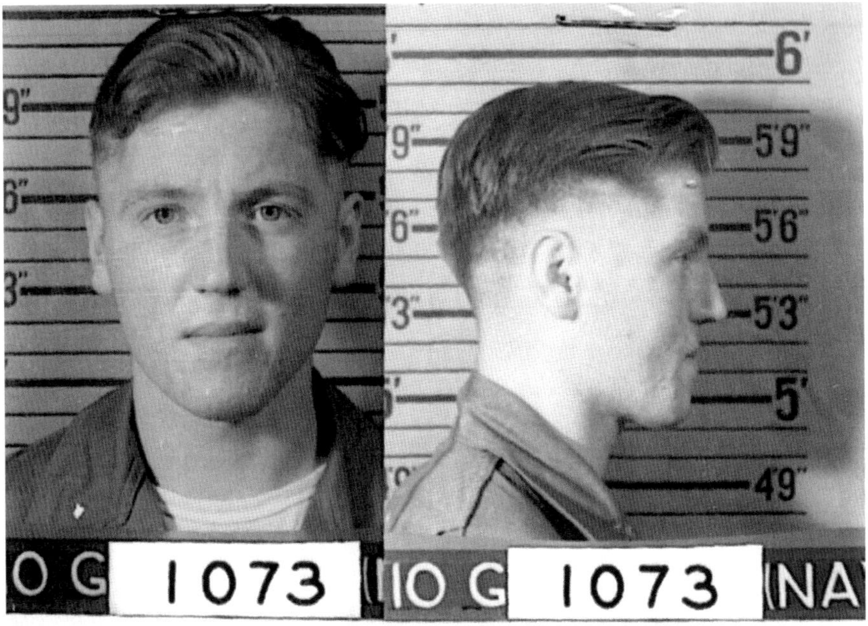

Guenther Kuelsen, a machinist on the *U-615*, rose to a position of leadership in the Hitler Youth Movement. *Courtesy National Archives, Washington, D.C.*

After Hox heard the testimony, he stared up at the ceiling and said, "There is nothing I can do personally, you know that, as I do not know the man personally. There is no official thing I can tell you to do or have done." Frustrated prisoners demanded advice on what they should do. Hox replied, "I can't advise you on that either. You have to figure that out for yourself. I leave that matter up to you." With that, he rose and left the room.

Otto Stengel returned to his barracks. While smoking a cigarette in his bunk, he brought his comrades up to date on the Drechsler situation. He told them that Drechsler would at least get the Holy Ghost and probably would not survive the night. Stengel's comrades bombarded him with questions, and he could not sleep. He got up and visited Drechsler's barracks ostensibly to ask about a friend from his hometown.

At first Drechsler was suspicious, but before long, he relaxed and talked freely. He showed Stengel bullet holes in his knee and neck to prove that he was not a traitor. Drechsler said his previous camp was much better than Camp Papago Park, which had hard cots, no radios and newspapers and restricted prisoner movements. "We had a newspaper printed in German."

Stengel countered that the so-called German newspaper was nothing more than an American propaganda publication printed by a German immigrant, which was true. "It insults our government, Dr. Goebbels, Hermann Goering and Adolf Hitler."[29]

Drechsler insisted that the paper printed the truth. "Hitler claimed that he did not want war, but then he got everyone involved in a war."

Stengel angrily protested, "I'm a good German, and I won't let you talk like that. Are you a German?" Drechsler ignored the question but instead asked, "Who do you think will win the war?" "Germany, of course." Drechsler then insisted that if Adolf Hitler, Hermann Goering and Joseph Goebbels had not been in power in Germany, there would be peace.

Stengel warned Drechsler, "Be careful what you say. I won't let you insult our government. We shall yet talk to each other tonight." He marched out and returned to his barracks.

To Rolf Wizuy, it was clear that Hox intended for them to kill Drechsler. Something had to be done about Drechsler immediately. Otherwise, he would go to the hospital in the morning and come under the protection of American authorities. The burden of his punishment rested on the shoulders of the enlisted soldiers against whom Drechsler's treason had been committed. Wizuy bitterly protested that there was only one right way to take care of the situation, and that was to hang Werner Drechsler. Murza and Elser suggested that the Holy Ghost might be sufficient for the moment because if they killed Drechsler it might endanger the entire camp. Wizuy argued that the Americans must have sent Drechsler to Camp Papago Park because they wanted him "taken care of."

He said, "If we give Drechsler the Holy Ghost, tomorrow he will be in another compound and will continue to harm Germany." Murza and Elser insisted that after the war, Drechsler would receive true justice. Wizuy argued that Drechsler might have been sent to Camp Papago Park to continue his espionage activities. Fischer, Kuelsen, Franke, Reyak and Ludwig all agreed with Wizuy. Others drifted off into the darkness of the night and wisely removed themselves from involvement in the Werner Drechsler murder.

About eight thirty that evening, several Germans passed the death sentence on Drechsler. Someone asked, "Who will carry out the execution?" Six men—Ludwig, Kuelsen, Wizuy, Fischer, Franke and Reyak—offered their services. In parting, Murza cautioned the executioners to be very careful about leaving fingerprints.[30] Wizuy, Fischer, Kuelsen, Franke and Reyak assembled in front of Compound 3 between the First Company orderly room and Compound 4, where Drechsler had already gone to bed. They discussed methods by which they could entice Drechsler out of his barracks. Wizuy proposed using a noncommissioned officer whom Drechsler had not yet met to lure him out of the building. At about nine o'clock, Fischer appeared with a tent rope tied into a crude noose. The rest distributed the gloves stolen from the infirmary. Fischer, Reyak and Ludwig prepared the noose in the shower room. The execution squad waited in silence until the lights in Drechsler's barracks went out.

At 9:15 p.m., Wizuy, Kuelsen and Franke reported that they had no luck in persuading any of the noncommissioned officers, including Murza, Hox, Elser and Reinl, to help them. They knew it was almost hopeless to get any assistance from the officers even though they wanted Drechsler put down. They made one last try by appealing to Friedrich Guggenberger to help them, but he ignored them. His awards included the Iron Cross with Oak Leaves. Guggenberger, born in Munich on March 6, 1915, joined the navy by 1934. Guggenberger was awarded the Oak Leaves to his Knight's Cross on January 31, 1943, at Hitler's headquarters in Rastenburg. He returned to sea in May 1943 in command of *U-513*. It was sunk on July 19, 1943, by depth charges from an American ship off the coast of Brazil. Guggenberger, one of seven survivors, was wounded and spent a day aboard a life raft before being picked up by an American ship, *Barnegat*. Guggenberger was operated on and then hospitalized before being transferred to Fort Hunt on September 25, 1943, and later moved to Camp Papago Park in late January 1944. Guggenberger made a second escape attempt with twenty-five U-boat prisoners through the *faustball* tunnel on December 24, 1944. The first time, he was captured in Tucson. The second time, he was recaptured near the Mexican border. After his repatriation to Germany, Guggenberger became an architect. He returned to the United States to study at the Naval War College in Rhode Island. He became the deputy chief of staff in the NATO command for four years. He disappeared while on a walk before traveling to the United States for a meeting of the Papago Trackers. Two years later, his body was found in the forest.[31]

They decided to take Drechsler out by force. Prisoners milled around Drechsler's barracks. Lights in the barracks remained on until ten o'clock, when a master switch threw the camp into darkness. Guard tower lights, which burned constantly, illuminated the barbed-wire fences but did not reach into the compound itself. Through this ghostly tableau, Otto Stengel moved from one group to another, always listening.

As the executioners approached the barracks, they were stopped by Stengel, who asked, "What are you going to do with Drechsler?"

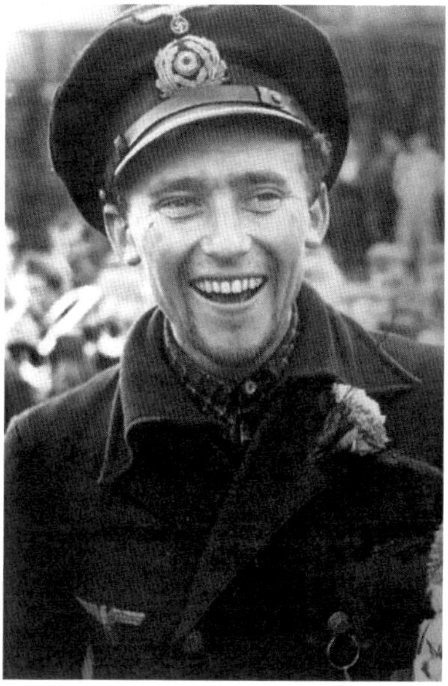

Friedrich Guggenberger ignored the pleas for help regarding what they should do about Werner Drechsler at Camp Papago Park. *Courtesy of Captain Jerry Mason's (Retd.) U boat Archive.*

Someone replied, "Kill him."

"How will you do this?"

"Hang him."

After complimenting them on their decision, Stengel asked how they were going to get Drechsler out of the barracks. When they said that they would drag him out, Stengel asked, "Do you need another man?"

Wizuy replied, "Yes, we could use one."

Stengel then made the worst decision of his life to join them. Now they were seven. Fischer, Kuelsen, Wizuy and Ludwig entered Drechsler's barracks from the front door; Reyak, Franke and Stengel came in through the rear. The group met at Drechsler's bunk. None of the prisoners acknowledged the entrants or got out of their bunks. Drechsler appeared to be sound asleep when the seven angry men, bent on murder, surrounded him. One of the Germans shook Drechsler by the shoulder.

"What's going on?"

A voice replied, "What the hell do you think is going on? What did you do to us in Washington?"

Drechsler squinted at Wizuy. "Please let me explain."

"You are a traitor."

Drechsler protested, "No, that is not true. Just wait until tomorrow morning. Then I will explain everything, and you will see what a mistake you are making."

"Tomorrow you will be with your American friends," someone snarled. Voices echoed, "You bastard, you betrayed Germany. We know what you did."

Drechsler cried, "No, it is not true."

The prisoners were disgusted by what Fischer described as cowardice. "You haven't cried before, admit that you turned traitor."

Drechsler pleaded, "I can explain, comrades. Give me until tomorrow. Please, comrades, I will tell you everything." His use of the word *kameraden*, or comrades, sent the seven men into a murderous frenzy.

They shouted, "You have no comrades, you bastard."

Then they pounced on Drechsler. Wizuy and Stengel grabbed Drechsler's legs while other hands reached for his arms and neck. Drechsler reacted with a strength born of terror. He gave Wizuy such a hard kick that it sent him flying across the floor. When Stengel lost his grip on the other leg, Drechsler staggered to his feet. Fists flew, and men crashed into the next bunk. The prisoner moved out of the path of the fatal struggle. Drechsler stood in the center of the aisle until three men grabbed him again. Even after a prisoner's jabbing fist smashed his face, he continued to fight for his life with an almost superhuman ferocity. Blood gushed out of his nostrils. A knee jammed into his groin and stunned him into immobility with a shock of excruciating pain. Someone stuffed a handkerchief into his mouth so he could not scream. The executioners dragged Drechsler outside.

Reyak noticed an American patrol jeep approaching the barracks and shouted, "The patrol jeep is coming. Wait!" They dumped Drechsler into the yard and fled. Drechsler regained consciousness and screamed. The American patrol jeep came to a complete stop. Its search light scanned the grounds, and the tower searchlight bore down on the group, which scattered.

Drechsler got to his feet and screamed, "Come on, if you have the courage." The jeep went on its way. Drechsler staggered back into his barracks with blood dripping down his face.

Reyak and Wizuy suggested that Drechsler had gotten a severe beating and that had to be enough for now. Stengel insisted that they finish him off. He argued that Drechsler could identify his assailants and would tell the Americans what had happened. All of the prisoners except Reyak agreed to go back.

Stengel argued, "We must do it together."

Reyak agreed to stay. They reentered the barracks. This time, Franke had a dog leash, which he tightened around Drechsler's neck so that he could not scream. Fischer stuffed a handkerchief in his mouth. Drechsler tried to stop the flow of blood and pleaded with them to wait until morning. He was weaker, but he still put up a fight. When Fischer stuffed the handkerchief in his mouth, Drechsler bit the middle finger of Fischer's right hand.

Fischer cursed, "Damn it, my finger is between his teeth."

Stengel gouged his thumb into Drechsler's throat. Another powerful kick in Drechsler's groin stunned him, and his screams of agony tapered into low, gurgling moans. Franke slipped the leash around his neck. Reyak held the door open while the executioners marched in an eerie double-time goose step as they carried Drechsler to the shower room. In an ironic effort to

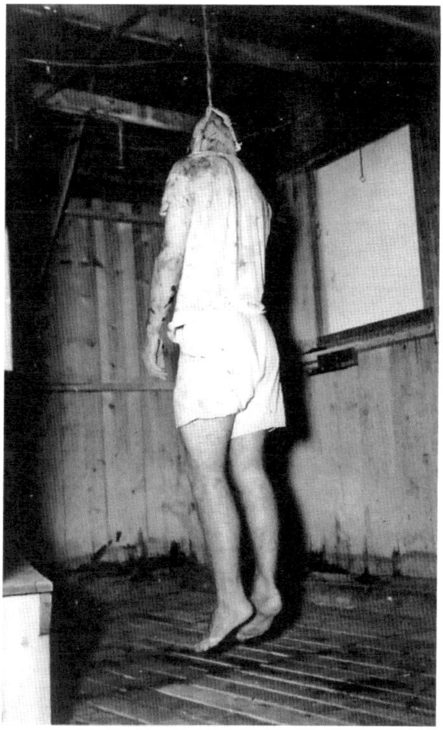

Werner Drechsler was discovered hanging from a bathroom rafter. His stay at Camp Papago Park had lasted just under seven hours. *Courtesy National Archives, Washington, D.C.*

keep him alive, every few steps Franke would loosen the leash to let him have some air. As soon as he revived, he tightened the noose again.

Reyak snarled at crowds of prisoners, "You had better get out of here."

He sat down and waited until he heard a bench topple over. Inside, the executioners had propped Drechsler up under the noose. Two of them jumped up on a bench, and the other four passed Drechsler up to them. One man steadied Drechsler while another slipped the rope around his neck and tightened it. When the noose was secure, the men kicked the bench from under their victim. It was almost ten o'clock. Werner Drechsler's stay at Camp Papago Park had lasted just under seven hours.

Just as Reyak reached the shower room, the executioners came out. Someone said, "It's over. It's finished now. You stay here, you have nothing to do in there."

Reyak watched Drechsler swaying in the eerie light, his feet about eight inches from the floor. The executioners returned to their barracks, where they cleaned up before going to their bunks. Stengel's bunk mates asked all at once, "How did it happen?"

When Stengel gave them details, they asked, "How is it that you know it so exactly?"

Stengel replied, "I myself participated in the crime." Then he went to sleep.

The next morning, the whistle blasted reveille. It was an ordinary day at Camp Papago Park except that no one used the shower room in Compound 4. Before long, it was common knowledge that Drechsler was hanging from a rafter in that room.

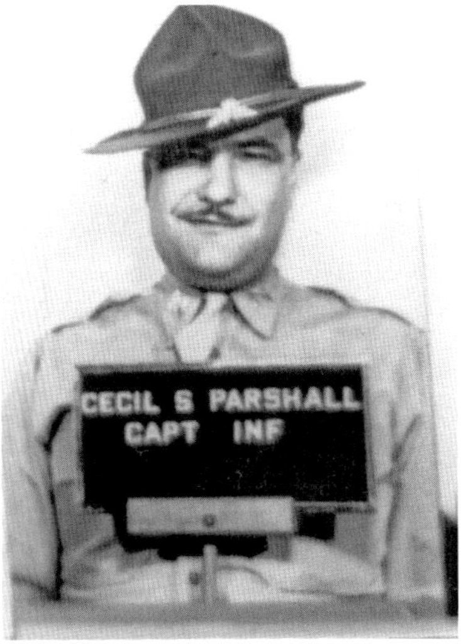

Provost Marshal Cecil Parshall served as acting commander of Camp Papago Park during the Werner Drechsler hanging. *Courtesy National Archives, Washington, D.C.*

Private Kenneth Brown, who discovered Drechsler's corpse, informed the camp's provost marshal, Captain Cecil Parshall, who was in his quarters shaving, of Drechsler's death. Brown explained, "It was not a suicide, Sir. It was murder."[32]

Parshall rushed off to Compound 4 with officers and staff members. After Parshall inspected the body, he posted a guard to keep anyone from entering and disturbing evidence. Parshall notified everyone who had a need to know, all the way up to the camp commander, of the murder. Sergeant Fred Bornstein and Captain Leland Hebblewaithe cut Drechsler's body down and placed it on a litter after photographing the body. The body was removed to Mortensen and Kingsley's mortuary in Phoenix. Hebblewaithe obtained three fingerprints off the right hand, the minimum required to meet legal identification requirements. He also confiscated the rope and tied it into an unusual knot to make it identifiable. At the mortuary, Captain Claude Stafford, Camp Papago Park's chief of surgical service, assisted by post physician Captain Max Marks, performed an autopsy on Drechsler the next day.

At reveille the next morning, the POWs were ordered to hold out their hands. As the inspectors moved closer to Fischer, other men changed places with him, to the amusement of the prisoners. He passed the inspection. Most of the prisoners knew who had participated in the murder, so the seven executioners counted on their comrades not to break down and reveal their desperate secret. Orders came from Wattenberg that no one in the compound was to admit knowing anything about Werner Drechsler. Means, who was under pressure over the hanging and several other incidents, appointed a committee of officers to conduct the investigation. Both the Ninth Services Command headquarters and Washington exerted pressure for a speedy resolution, but after two weeks, they were no closer to an answer than they had been on March 13. By April, the executioners began to feel secure.

Prisoners were sent to work as though nothing had happened. Over the next few weeks, about one hundred German POWs were interrogated. When asked about Drechsler's murder, Wattenberg coldly replied, "I don't know whether he was killed or whether he killed himself."

Years later, he would remark that it was an incident of no importance. Prisoners, fearful for their lives, fingered Wattenberg, and it was not long before they began contradicting one another. Although Wattenberg insisted that he had no contact with the German prisoners during the hanging, several prisoners testified that on the Sunday afternoon when Drechsler arrived, the captain exhorted them to be good soldiers. Oskar Meyer heard him say, "Here among us are quite a few who do not think as we do and these people must, under the circumstances, be taken care of so that they can't talk anymore."[33]

Fischer confessed that he heard the captain say that he was glad that Drechsler was dead and "these people that are still here, these anti-Nazis, they should be encircled and the noose put around their necks." Johann Neumair heard Wattenberg urge the executioners to wear gloves so they would not scratch themselves. He warned the prisoners that any German who did not stick with the Germans and who worked for the Americans or who gave evidence of being anti-Nazi should be weeded out and given a good beating. "The one who is a traitor to his fatherland, it is not worthwhile for him to live."[34] Guenther Albert corroborated Neumair's statement and testified that he believed that Wattenberg had given the order to kill Drechsler. Albert was later transferred out of Camp Papago Park because of his anti-Nazi attitudes.[35]

Within a month, the army had focused on twenty suspects, who were transferred to a secret camp near Stockton, California. The questioning methods were classified and have never been fully revealed, but it is known that they were brutal and effective. A noncommissioned officer, Friedrich Murza, was the first to crack. He claimed that after the prisoners discovered Drechsler's identity as a traitor, they decided to kill him. He was terrified because if he were to be returned to Camp Papago Park, his compatriots would guess that he had implicated others to free himself. If he did not talk, the Americans might indict him.

Ultimately, Murza and noncommissioned officer Sigfried Elser named the seven men—Fritz Franke, Bernhard Reyak, Guenther Kuelsen, Otto Stengel, Heinrich Ludwig, Helmut Fischer and Rolf Wizuy—who would be found guilty of Drechsler's murder.[36] In the final charges, the names of Elser and Murza were dropped. In all likelihood, they fingered others to save their own lives. When confronted with the evidence, each man confessed but insisted that he had punished a traitor as an act of war, not committed murder. On June 30, Colonel Gerald L. Church, Major Francis P. Walsh and Major Herman J. Zabel reported that German prisoner of war Werner Drechsler came to his death by strangulation on the night of Sunday, March 12, 1944, at 9:30 p.m. at Camp Papago Park, Phoenix, Arizona, and that Werner Drechsler had been murdered by hanging by German prisoners of war Otto Stengel, Rolf Wizuy, Heinrich Ludwig, Helmut Fischer, Fritz Franke, Bernhard Reyak and Guenther Kuelsen. German prisoners of war Sigfried Elser and Friedrich Murza also aided and assisted, counseled and advised the murderers of Drechsler prior to such murder and, therefore, should be charged and tried as accessories before the fact. The board recommended that these prisoners be charged and tried for the murder of Werner Drechsler under the provisions of Article of War 92.

On July 11, 1944, the Ninth Service Command issued an order signed by Colonel John H. Wilson, chief of staff of Ninth Service Command, to convene a general court-martial for these prisoners. The board found that these prisoners of war, jointly and in pursuance of a common intent, did with malice aforethought, willfully, deliberately, feloniously and with premeditation, kill Werner Drechsler by strangulation.[37]

CHAPTER 4

CONFESSIONS AND COURT-MARTIAL

Murza was recalled again, and Church asked if the men were wearing gloves. Murza said they were and that he was prepared to swear to it. Church then insisted that Murza tell the whole story again for the record. The second time around, Murza implicated Helmut Fischer along with Wizuy, Mandelkow, Nieswand, Ludwig and Polowzyk. Church went over the statements and forced Murza to admit that he had previously lied. At eleven thirty that evening, he was returned to his cell and collapsed on his cot. Church now had a confession and implication of other prisoners.

After Murza's confession, the board reconvened and proceeded to pressure the others for confessions. Stengel admitted that he had participated in beating and hanging Drechsler and described the crime in great detail. He only knew Wizuy by name and could not identify the others. After he joined the execution squad, they went to Drechsler's compound, where he took Drechsler's legs while the others grabbed his arms from each side. Drechsler broke free and attacked one of his assailants. The POW who had been sleeping on the bunk next to Drechsler moved so as not to involve himself in the fight. Stengel described the fight as rough and made a moving justification, stating that he had committed an act of war, not murder, because Drechsler had been a traitor. Some of Stengel's family lost their lives during the war, including a female cousin who was killed in a bombing attack. He thought that if he were to be placed before a court-martial he would stand before soldiers who would understand his course of action. "I have made this statement because during the entire time in my room the picture was in front of my eyes of how Drechsler was hanging there."

When Stengel's oral confession was complete, Church directed that he be put in an isolated cell and provided with pen and paper so that he could record his confession in his own handwriting. This procedure was followed with all seven prisoners. Zabel composed and dictated the addenda to each confession stating that the confession was voluntary without any offer of reward, threats, promises or duress.[38]

Church called in Siegfried Elser, who broke down when he sensed that the world was closing in on him. He was reminded that he was under oath and questioned about his activities on March 12, 1944. He stated that Rudolf Weimer entered Drechsler's barracks with another man but that Drechsler was already asleep.

Elser said, "Thereupon I suggested that the matter be postponed until the next day and I retired from the group."

The group milling around Drechsler's barracks grew to about forty, and they were discussing removing Drechsler by force. Elser confirmed that the testimony that he had given at Camp Papago Park on April 22, when he said that he knew nothing about the murder, was a lie. At some point, Elser decided to participate in killing Drechsler because he had gotten a pair of gloves. Finally, a very nervous Elser claimed that the purpose of the gloves was to conceal evidence and he was afraid of excluding himself from the group but denied that he got them to help hang Drechsler. After intensive questioning by Zabel, he denied being in favor of hanging Drechsler but admitted that he was in favor of beating him up. He claimed that most of the prisoners thought Drechsler should be hanged.

Zabel informed Elser that even though he contended that he only wanted to see Drechsler beaten, "you being a participant, a planner of that particular action, you are also a participant in the hanging of Drechsler." Seeing that Elser was shaken, the board reminded him that he and Murza were ranking noncommissioned officers and that enlisted men followed their lead.

Word was passed to "Captain Oscar Schmidt" to intensify his interrogation of Rolf Wizuy. Despite specific and harsh interrogation, Wizuy denied any knowledge of the murder. When he broke down and admitted to his participation, he said that he believed that the board knew of his connection and that he had been implicated by others. Wizuy described his meeting with Drechsler in Washington, D.C., wherein Drechsler tried to get him to talk about Germany and his ship, but Wizuy did not trust him. At Camp Papago Park, Wizuy talked with some of his buddies about Drechsler and what should be done with a traitor. In his confession, he implicated Helmut Fischer, Fritz Franke, Bernhard Reyak, Guenther Kuelsen, Friedrich Murza, Siegfried Elser and Heinrich Ludwig but cleared Guenther Bleise, who returned to his work in the canteen.[39] Wizuy told the board that they should understand that when the Germans saw Drechsler in Camp Papago Park, they were certain that he did not arrive there by accident. He thought the Americans wanted Drechsler eliminated, but he thought that a beating was enough. However, Stengel took over command of the group and insisted on hanging Drechsler.

"Schmidt" interrogated him all day and well into the night. "Schmidt" and "Sgt. Paul Held" spelled each other. The real identity of these two men has not been discovered. A little before eight o'clock the next morning, a weary, trembling Wizuy informed "Schmidt" that he was ready to confess and wanted to be taken before the board. He told his story in extensive detail from first hearing about Drechsler's arrival to washing his gloves after the heinous act was complete. He admitted that he wanted to see Drechsler hanged because he personally knew him as a traitor. In an isolated cell, he wrote out his confession, which stated, "I want to add at this time that the crime probably will be considered by the court-martial judges as a bloody deed, but I want to state emphatically that we considered the crime as a military action, and that we had to break the resistance of Drechsler."

After the board finished, Wizuy, who had worked in the kitchen throughout the investigation, handed his confession to Zabel and asked, "How does the major feel about being waited upon by a murderer at Camp Papago Park?"[40]

Later, on June 3, Heinrich Ludwig confessed to his part in the murder and implicated the same persons as Wizuy.[41] He added that Werner Reinl had warned the men not to act in haste.[42] According to Ludwig, after the meeting with Hox, the men met outside and either Elser, Murza or Reinl asked, "Who wants to participate in it?"

Kuelsen, Franke, Fischer, Wizuy, Reyak and Ludwig volunteered for the executioners' squad. The ensuing discussion centered on whether to beat up or hang Drechsler. Ludwig admitted that his original story denying participation in the crime had been a lie. Walsh asked who wanted Drechsler beat up and who wanted him hanged. Ludwig said that Murza and Elser wanted him beat up, but others said that then Drechsler would go to the Americans with their names so he should be hanged. The others did not break easily, but by June 8, Franke, Kuelsen, Reyak and finally Fischer had confessed.[43] The board continued to work on Murza, Elser, Paul Buchholz, Lothar Mandelkow, Walter Niemann and Rudolf Weimer.

The court could not attach any of these POWs directly to the physical action of the hanging.

The men recalled that Hox convened a moot court and said, "I cannot do anything about this matter. You must know best what to do with Drechsler." Franke and Wizuy asked Werner Reinl and Josef Hoeller to get Drechsler to come out of his barracks and "we would take care of him."[44]

As they confessed, they began to justify their actions and explain how they had really not participated in the crime. Kuelsen had never met Drechsler until that fateful Sunday. On the soccer field, Drechsler told him that at the previous camp he was the only navy man in an army camp, which Kuelsen thought strange. During the court-martial, Kuelsen pleaded that he did not take part in the hanging and that just as he was to give them a hand, the crime was finished.

Reyak, who knew Drechsler as Leime in Washington, D.C., told how when Drechsler screamed, he closed the compound door and tried to disperse the gathering crowd. He claimed that by the time he got to the bathhouse, Drechsler was already hanging from the rafters. When asked why he had confessed, Reyak said it was because he had sworn to tell the whole truth and because he considered an oath "holy," and the worst crime he could commit would be to break an oath.

In Washington, D.C., Helmut Fischer learned that two Germans by the name of Leime and Weigel had deserted the German cause. Fischer was interrogated by a crew mate of Drechsler, Hans Wosnitzka, who operated under the name of Weigel. After the soccer game that Sunday, Fischer met Drechsler, who fitted the description of Wosnitzka's friend in Washington, D.C. Wosnitzka, one of many Polish men forced to choose between going into submarine service or being shot, told his interrogators that the German people were not getting enough to eat and hoped that the war would end soon. Wosnitzka appeared to be extremely cooperative and willing to answer all questions with the exception of providing the number of his U-boat. He was anxious to be kept completely separate from the other prisoners. Wosnitzka hated the Germans and wanted to help the United States by doing garden work and driving a car. With an equivalent of a high school education, he had previously worked as a shipping clerk. He had no friends or relatives in the United States, and after his rescue, he underwent surgery to repair numerous hemorrhages throughout his small intestines. While in the water, a bomb had exploded within twenty or thirty meters of him.

On June 20, the board made recommendations to the Department of War. The findings were signed by Colonel Church, Major Zabel and Major

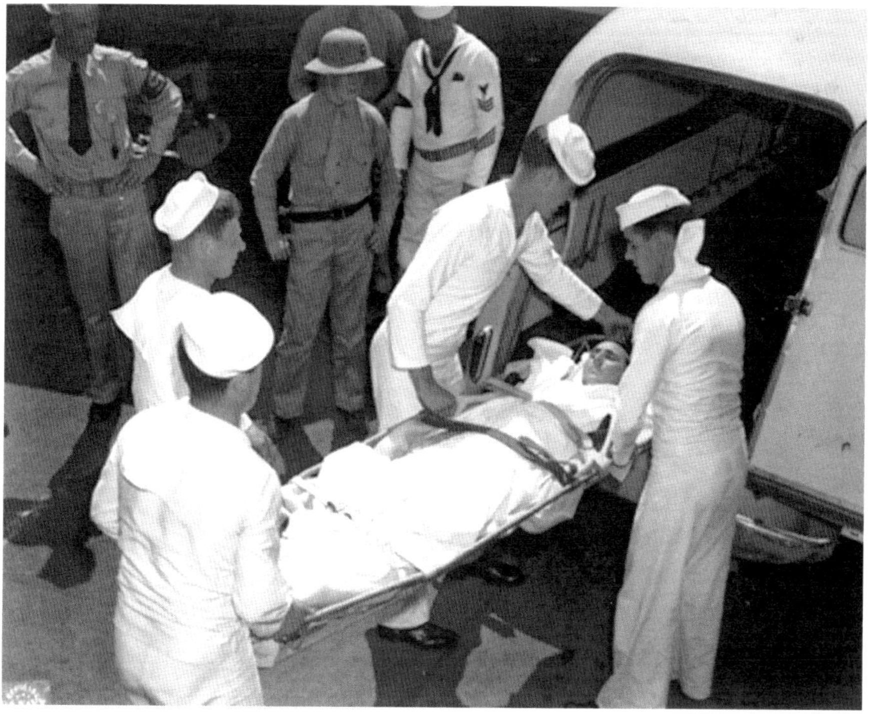

Hans Wosnitzka claimed to have aided the Americans during his capture. *Courtesy of Captain Jerry Mason's (Retd.) U-boat Archive.*

Walsh. It recommended that the following prisoners of war be charged with and tried for the willful and premeditated murder of Werner Drechsler: Otto Stengel, Rolf Wizuy, Heinrich Ludwig, Helmut Fischer, Fritz Franke, Bernhard Reyak and Guenther Kuelsen, and that the following prisoners of war be charged with and tried for the murder of Drechsler as accessories before the fact: Siegfried Elser and Friedrich Murza. Elser and Murza never came to trial. When Walsh learned of the investigating board's success, he was in Florence, Arizona, prosecuting an arson case against an Italian prisoner of war.

In Stockton, Walsh prepared the documents to be sent to the Ninth Services Command. The case produced problems involving early use of a lie detector test and the methods used to obtain the "voluntary" confessions on which Walsh had to base his prosecution. Church convened a board of officers to assist him. Major Herman J. Zabel became his assistant, and Major Francis P. Walsh of the Judge Advocate General Corps served as recorder. Zabel, born in 1894, had joined the U.S. Coast Guard in 1913.

A year later, he enlisted in the regular army. Fluent in German, he moved up quickly in the ranks during World War II. He retired and died in Phoenix in 1979. Walsh, in his forties, had a successful civil practice in San Francisco before the war broke out but had never tried a criminal case. Now he was about to try seven men for first-degree murder, and their conviction would carry the penalty of death by hanging. Sergeant Carl F. Blank, Captain Oscar Schmidt and Sergeant Paul Held served as interpreters. Sergeant Michael Donohue recorded the proceedings. Donohue was born in Bisbee and died in Douglas, Arizona. Schmidt and Held are aliases.

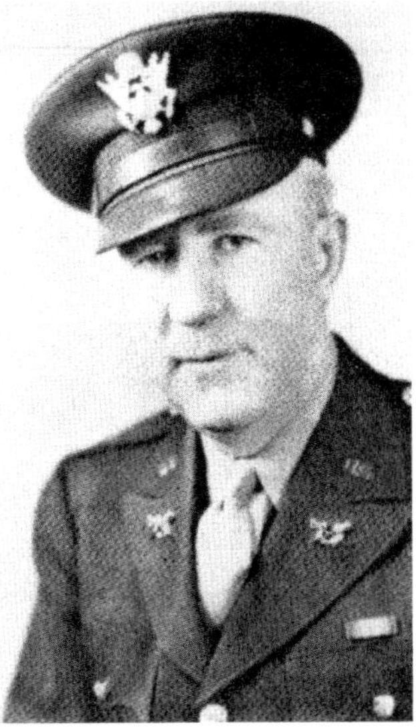

Francis Walsh served as both interrogator and prosecutor of Drechsler's executioners. *Courtesy National Archives, Washington, D.C.*

The board flew to Washington, D.C., to investigate Drechsler's activities while a prisoner there in hopes that they could link his murder with specific names at Camp Papago Park. The navy was disappointed in the manner in which the army had handled Drechsler, especially after it had warned the military about sending him to a camp that quartered U-boat submariners. However, the navy did provide the board with a list of Drechsler's crew mates from the *U-118*. Interrogations of the prisoners dragged on through the month of April. The accused were told that their American interrogators were not attempting to learn military secrets but only the truth about the murder of Werner Drechsler. All of the interrogations were prefaced by reading the Twenty-Fourth Article of War (see Appendix A).

On May 30, 1944, Church brought Leonarde Keeler, a lie detector expert from Chicago, to Camp Papago Park. Keeler, who developed the prototype of the modern polygraph machine with John Reid and Fred Inbau, tested everyone who might be remotely connected with the case. The polygraph measured the suspect's pulse, brain waves and perspiration. Keeler's questions focused on what the prisoners saw or heard on the night of the murder. The prisoners, including those in the bunks near Drechsler, insisted that they had neither heard nor seen anything and that they had chosen not to see the faces of the men who committed the crime. After each interrogation, Keeler reviewed the results of the test, and within a month, he had narrowed down the list of major suspects to twenty men.

The first to be questioned from Drechsler's ship was the senior noncommissioned officer Werner Reinl. Reinl was on bridge watch the day the *U-118* was destroyed. He admitted that everyone talked about Drechsler and that he had urged Franz Hox to at least listen to the complaints against Drechsler to determine whether there was anything to the rumors. Reinl claimed to be building a model ship the night Drechsler was hanged and that he had gone to bed about 9:00 p.m. The lie detector test indicated that Reinl was lying, and he was slated for recall, during which he admitted that he had made a list of names of those who had known Drechsler in Washington, D.C., that included Guenther Bleise, Heinrich Ludwig, Friedrich Murza, Siegfried Elser and Rolf Wizuy.

After the lights went out, Radioman First Class Josef Heller and Rolf Wizuy approached Reinl's bunk and said, "Mister Obermaat, would you go over to Drechsler's barracks and get him out?"

Reinl replied, "That is out of the question for me," and went to sleep.

Reinl denied being present during the moot court trial even though Hox had testified that he was present. Hox had been captured while serving under Captain Jurgen Wattenberg on the *U-162*. After several intense interrogations, he admitted to meeting with the prisoners regarding Werner Drechsler on the evening of the hanging. Several prisoners told him that they had roomed with Drechsler and that after he talked to them, he would report the conversations to the Americans.

Reinl told Hox, "Here seems to be a traitor. Everybody is excited, and you should report that to Captain Wattenberg." He then handed Hox the list and said, "These are the names of the men that Drechsler had been together with at the interrogation camp near Washington."

Hox claimed that the meeting was held at Camp Papago Park only to determine if Drechsler was a traitor and the results would be reported to Wattenberg. He insisted that there was no discussion about punishing Drechsler. Hermann Wiedemann saw Drechsler at the soccer game but did not speak to him. Rudolf Wiemer failed the lie detector test when questioned about the night of the murder. Wiemer, a noncommissioned officer from the *U-118*, testified that while he was in Washington, D.C., an American naval officer told him that Drechsler talked a lot. Wiemer said he did not believe that Drechsler was a traitor because he had been such a good submariner. During his recall, he said that when Drechsler arrived at Camp Papago Park, Herman Polowzyk had come into the barracks of the *U-118* crew and brought greetings from Drechsler. Later, he found Drechsler asleep. Wizuy had asked Wiemer to lure Drechsler out of the barracks, but Drechsler pretended to be asleep and would not wake up. Polowzyk was asked by Wizuy, Murza, Kuelsen, Fischer, Franke, Reyak and Ludwig to lure Drechsler out of the barracks so they could give him the Holy Ghost. Polowzyk said he and Wiemer went into the barracks, but Drechsler was sleeping very soundly.[45]

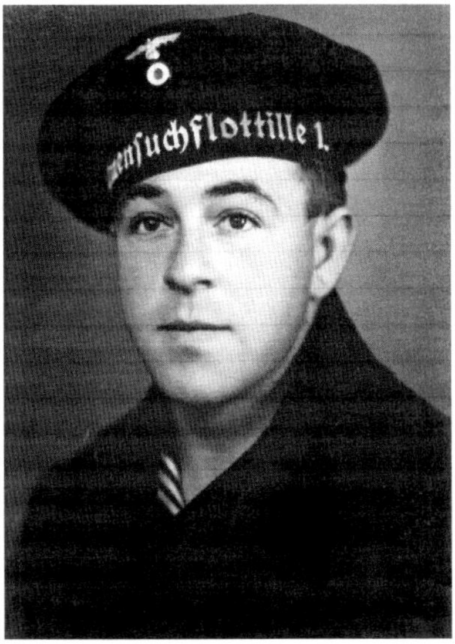

Werner Reinl claimed to be building a model ship the night Drechsler was hanged and said that he had gone to bed about 9:00 p.m. *Courtesy National Archives, Washington, D.C.*

Lothar Mandelkow failed the lie detector test when he said he knew nothing about Drechsler until after he was dead. Upon recall, he admitted that he had heard talk during the soccer game that Drechsler, whom he had known as a traitor under the name of Brabant, had arrived at Camp Papago Park. Mandelkow wanted to tell Hox that he had been with Drechsler in Washington, but his comrades told him, "Keep your hands off. There will only be trouble. Otherwise, you will probably be taken away sometime for an interrogation." When Hox issued a second call for those who knew Drechsler, Mandelkow appeared, but too late to testify. He heard someone say, "They are probably going to hang Drechsler. Come on! Let's go!" Later that night, Mandelkow learned that Drechsler had been hanged. Mandelkow and Polowzyk were the only prisoners to attend Drechsler's first burial at the Florence, Arizona cemetery.[46] Walter Nieswand, who testified that he knew nothing of Drechsler until the morning after the hanging, ultimately admitted that he had been summoned by Guenther Bleise to attend Hox's meeting. Nieswand, who had roomed with Drechsler in Washington, identified most of the prisoners at the meeting. He admitted to hearing screams coming from Drechsler's barracks, but when he tried to enter, he was turned away. After Drechsler was hanged, Nieswand went in to look at him.[47]

Guenther Bleise said he did not participate in the hanging because he and his comrades were enjoying a birthday party on the night of the hanging. He admitted to rounding up the men for Hox and identified them as Ludwig,

Buchholz, Wizuy, Mandelkow, Elser, Wagenfuehr, Nieswan and Fischer. He also identified a picture of Drechsler as the man he knew by the name of Limmer in Washington, D.C. Chief Warrant Officer and compound spokesman Joseph Gross told his interrogators that the American authorities should never have sent Drechsler to Camp Papago Park. He said, "If I had been there when this man was hung [*sic*], I would not have lifted one finger to stop it. Drechsler had hundreds of comrades' lives on his conscience, and every decent American soldier would have felt the same way."

Even though the lie detector tests proved that several prisoners were lying, the board knew that it needed confessions if it hoped to go to trial. An admission came from Alfred Friedrich, who lived in the same barracks as Otto Stengel. Friedrich admitted that he knew who killed Drechsler but would not tell the board unless he was given permission by Wattenberg. Church told Wattenberg that one prisoner knew who was involved in Drechsler's murder and would give out the names if he had Wattenberg's permission. As to be expected, Wattenberg absolutely refused. Friedrich was recalled for additional questioning. When the board demanded that he tell who had said that Drechsler was a traitor who should be hanged, Friedrich quietly replied, "Stengel, Otto Stengel." Friedrich said that when he asked Stengel how he knew so much about the hanging and who did it, Stengel laughed and said, "I don't know." When several prisoners reacted with horror at Stengel's description of the beating, he insisted that Drechsler deserved much more. Friedrich admitted that he had seen blood on Stengel's face when he washed up after the murder. When Captain Hebblewaithe told the prisoners that fingerprints had been taken from Drechsler's neck, which was a lie, Stengel remembered that he had forgotten to wear gloves.

The next day, Church called Otto Stengel as a witness. Stengel described how he had sought Drechsler out and their subsequent conversation. When he tried to enter Drechsler's barracks, Elser and Murza stopped him, whispering, "Something is happening here." Stengel returned to his barracks, but his bunk mates wanted more details. Stengel told Walsh that he was the source of information for his barracks, and Walsh said, "You mean you are a gossip?" Walsh pressed him for names of the men who murdered Drechsler, but Stengel said he could not tell him because the lower parts of their faces were covered with handkerchiefs. Murza identified Drechsler as a traitor who went by the name of Niemmer and who had roomed with him in Washington. Later he learned that the man he knew as Niemmer was actually Drechsler, who had asked him questions about his U-boat. Murza testified that Niemmer did not act right at Fort Meade and had a wound scar on his right knee. Murza told his interrogators that he saw men wash blood off their surgical gloves and that Fischer had refused a medical examination because Drechsler had bitten his thumb. Murza became a prime suspect when the lie detector test showed that he had told the truth about Fischer's injured thumb. When Murza was recalled, he testified that when Drechsler came out of the mess hall, he had told Guenther Bleise, "That is him!" Bleise ordered him to report to Hox. Murza testified that besides himself, Siegfried Elser, Guenther Bleise, Lothar Mandelkow, Rolf Wizuy, Heinrich Ludwig, Herman Polowzyk and Walter Nieswand were present at the meeting. Murza advised that Drechsler should be beaten up, and while some agreed, others, including Wizuy, insisted that "a complete job will be done." Under more intense interrogation, Murza admitted that he recognized Helmut Fischer and Rolf Wizuy carrying Drechsler out of the barracks but claimed that he could not identify the others. Rolf Wizuy failed his lie detector test and, when confronted with the results, admitted that he knew that the man by the name of Leimi at Fort Meade was Drechsler. He insisted that he and Drechsler just had friendly conversations and did not discuss military information. When asked if he knew would he tell them, he replied, "No."

Johann Matzke, born in Poland, immigrated to Germany in 1915. He was serving on a blockade runner when he was captured by the Americans in the south Atlantic. On the evening of March 12, he learned that one of his bunk mates had been hanged as a traitor. He went to have a look, but Stengel told him to go away. When Matzke asked if Ludwig had been involved in hanging Drechsler, Ludwig only shrugged his shoulders and asked, "What should I do? How should I conduct myself?" After Matzke returned from his last interrogation session, Ludwig told him, "If I am called out now, know who has given away my name."[48] On the night of the murder, Rudi Stressel, one of the first prisoners at Camp Papago Park, and his friends listened to another prisoner sing for a while. Suddenly, they heard screams coming from Drechsler's barracks, but they stayed where they were. From their door, they saw five men, stepping in double time, carrying a body out of Drechsler's barracks. He insisted that he could not identify any of the men.

Lieutenant Hermann Ritter, an officer quartered with Wattenberg, spoke fluent English and testified that he had never been a Nazi. The forty-five-year-old Roman Catholic Ritter, born in Munich to a Finnish mother and Austrian father, had been captured on a trawler off the coast of Greenland by the Danes, who turned him over to the Americans. He testified that Wattenberg and the other officers thought the hanging of Drechsler was "all right."

Walsh asked Ritter why he requested a transfer out of Camp Papago Park. Ritter said that at Crossville, Tennessee, Wattenberg had suspected him of being a spy when he spoke to Americans. The captain told the other prisoners, "This Ritter, I don't believe he is an officer. The Americans put him in our camp as a spy." Ritter told the board that Wattenberg tried to have a non-Nazi German hanged at Crossville, and now Ritter feared for his life. Wattenberg had said "that every officer would be annihilated who showed weakness and didn't agree and didn't show the Nazi spirit." When asked if Wattenberg knew who hanged Drechsler, Ritter replied, "I know that Wattenberg is inspirational to hanging people up."

By the end of April, sixteen men had been singled out for intensive interrogation: Alfred Friedrich, Friedrich Murza, Siegfried Elser, Werner Reinl, Rudolf Wiemer, Herman Polowzyk, Rolf Wizuy, Otto Stengel, Helmut Fischer, Heinrich Ludwig, Guenther Kuelsen, Fritz Franke, Bernhard Reyak, Walter Newlands, Gerhard Richter and Lothar Mandelkow. These prime suspects were removed from their barracks and placed in the stockade at Camp Papago Park.

Within a few days, the investigating board decided to remove the prisoners to a secret camp near Modesto, California, which was used primarily for interrogating Japanese residents who were suspected of being in sympathy with the enemy. The camp had a well-known reputation for culling confessions. On May 3, the prisoners as a group were taken to California, where they were placed in cells on the second floor of a jail. All the suspects were kept in solitary confinement and held incommunicado. Their cells were bugged, and an operator manned the monitors twenty-four hours a day. Interrogations were conducted by "Captain Oscar Schmidt" and "Sergeant Paul Held." The real identities of these two men were known to only a few and were never disclosed, even during the court-martial. Their methods were, to say the least, brutal and effective. Torture involved putting a gas mask on a prisoner and clogging it with an onion or a garlic clove. Prisoners were blindfolded and driven around at high rates of speed with a metal bar weaving back and forth inside the car. Schmidt shoved Stengel's exposed genitalia against a steaming radiator. By the end of May, everything had fallen into place for a court-martial.

The interrogations took their toll on the prisoners. Gerhard Richter, a loyal Nazi, failed miserably on the lie detector test. He had been with Drechsler at Fort Meade and roomed with Otto Stengel at Camp Papago Park. Richter, by far the most belligerent Nazi, completely cracked under questioning. He testified that during the soccer game, the prisoners heard Stengel say that Drechsler should be hanged. That evening when Stengel returned to the barracks, he announced, "Do you know that the traitor is already hung [*sic*]?" When asked who else heard Stengel's announcement, Richter replied, "Anybody who was not asleep." Richter admitted that he lied to the board at Camp Papago Park because he did not want to involve Stengel, who had a wife and two small children. The guard dismissed Richter and recalled a thoroughly frightened Alfred Friedrich.

The board bore down hard, questioning Friedrich in detail about Stengel. Friedrich said that Stengel told how Drechsler tried to defend himself. Friedrich then tried to soften his accusation of Stengel and said, "I cannot say for certain that Stengel did it." Friedrich was removed, and Otto Stengel was brought in for additional interrogation.

Stengel admitted that he was in the vicinity, but only as a spectator. He testified that when he arrived, Drechsler was lying on the ground, and he noticed that someone had kicked him. When asked what he did next, Stengel described the removal and beating of Drechsler and the ultimate hanging but insisted that he with "200 or 300 other prisoners" went over to the shower only to observe Drechsler's body. When Church questioned him about fingerprints, Stengel became visibly agitated. He was sent back to his cell, and "Captain Schmidt" was given orders to put pressure on him.

Murza, a high-ranking suspect, was involved, but the board did not know the extent. "Schmidt" interrogated him off and on for almost twenty-four hours, and on the evening of June 1, he was brought before Church and Zabel. The frightened, tired Murza was reminded that he was still under oath. He explained that when he came out of the movie that Sunday afternoon, he was told by Wiedemann from *U-118* that Drechsler was in camp. When Drechsler came out of the mess hall, Murza pointed and said, "That is him." He said it to all those who were with him. When asked who else was there, Murza replied wearily that the group included Bleise, Ludwig, Wizuy, Elser, Mandelkow and several prisoners who he did not know. He thought two other members from the *U-118*, Werner Reinl and Herman Polowzyk, were present. Murza, by now weak and tired, described the meeting with Franz Hox. Two groups formed outside. In the first were Elser, Bleise and Mandelkow. In the second group were Wizuy, Ludwig, Nieswand and Polowzyk. Under the relentless probing of Church, the events of that Sunday evening were reconstructed. Murza, along with Siegfried Elser, Rudolf Weimer and several others, marched over to the barracks.

Elser had been a Catholic until 1932, when he joined the Hitler Youth Movement. He, too, had met Drechsler at Fort Meade. Under Church's probing, Elser described how he watched the men drag Drechsler out of the barracks, how Drechsler had fought back and how the men fled under the glare of spotlights. Murza was recalled, and Church asked if the men were wearing gloves. Murza was prepared to swear that they were. Church insisted that Murza tell the whole story again for the record. The second time around, Murza implicated Helmut Fischer along with Wizuy, Mandelkow, Nieswand, Ludwig and Polowzyk. Weimer had taken no part in the actual beating. Church went over the statements and forced Murza to admit that he had previously lied. At 11:30 that evening, he was returned to his cell and collapsed on his cot. Church and Zabel knew that for the first time in more than two months they had direct implication of three men in the actual hanging: Otto Stengel, Rolf Wizuy and Helmut Fischer. Still, uncorroborated testimony linked Walter Nieswand, Herman Polowzyk, Lothar Mandelkow, Heinrich Ludwig and Rudolf Weimer to the crime.

As a result, Walsh decided to send an investigating officer to each of the accused and give them an opportunity to reconsider their confessions. The Judge Advocate General Office assigned Lieutenant Harry A. Baldwin as investigating officer. The prisoners were removed from Stockton and incarcerated at various army facilities in California. Stengel was taken to Dibble General Hospital at Menlo Park, where he was operated on for appendicitis on June 5. He was given a neuropsychiatric examination and judged to be cooperative and showed no evidence of mental disease. He understood the nature of his acts and was able to distinguish right from wrong. Wizuy was quartered at Hammond General Hospital in Modesto. Ludwig was taken to DeWitt General Hospital at Auburn. Fischer, Franke, Kuelsen and Reyak were held separately at a rehabilitation center in Turlock. They had a month to recuperate from their ordeal before Baldwin appeared for questioning. Baldwin drove to Dibble General Hospital on July 3 to question Stengel, who was ambulatory and brought to a room where Baldwin waited with two staff sergeants, Melvin Oboe as reporter and "Paul Held" as interpreter. Each time he told the prisoner:

> *I am investigating the hanging of Prisoner of War Werner Drechsler which occurred on or about 12 or 13 March 1944 in Compound 4, Camp Papago Park, Phoenix, Arizona. Under Article of War 70, and as a German prisoner of war, you are entitled to the protection of the Articles of War. I am not the prosecutor, nor do I represent the prosecution. I am not your counsel. I am here merely to inquire into the truth of the charges and to recommend what disposition should be made in the interest of justice and discipline.*[49]

When Baldwin was convinced that Stengel understood his purpose, he read the charge and the specification against him. Baldwin followed these procedures with each of the seven prisoners, and they were given the opportunity to examine the evidence against them and refute their previous confessions. Each prisoner was advised, "You have the right to remain silent at this time and say nothing, or you have the right to present anything in your own behalf in defense or mitigation. You have the right to make a statement in any form, subject, however, to its being used against you in the future. Do you understand?"[50]

Stengel became especially interested when Baldwin read the list of witnesses against him, and he specifically asked to hear the testimony of Alfred Friedrich. Stengel said that Friedrich told him in the Camp Florence guardhouse that he hoped the murderers would be caught soon because he wanted to go back to Camp Papago Park. Friedrich promised never to give away Stengel's name, but when Stengel heard the testimony, he saw that Friedrich had implicated him several times. Stengel added that he participated in Drechsler's murder because Drechsler was a traitor and that he had acted like any German soldier. Baldwin read Stengel Articles of War Twenty-Four and Seventy, which dealt with prohibited self-incrimination and the necessity for an impartial investigation of the charges. Stengel then made a statement in his own defense. He had told his friends that Drechsler would not survive until the next day and that he would get the Holy Ghost that evening. "At first I did not think that I would get involved in the crime, in spite of the fact that the hatred against Drechsler was pretty intense because he had insulted Adolph Hitler and my government in the worst way possible." Drechsler had insisted that if Hitler, Hermann Goering and Joseph Goebbels had not been in power in Germany, there would be peace. Stengel's temper flared, and he said, "Be careful what you say. I am a German, and I won't let you insult our government." Stengel told the board how they had discussed the idea that most of the POWs thought that the enemy (Americans) liked treason but had no respect for the traitor. His personal reasons for killing Drechsler were that he had on his conscience German wives and children, thousands of brave submariners and possibly Stengel's female cousin who was killed in a bombing attack on Berlin, as well as the sister of Stengel's wife, who lost her home when American bombs destroyed everything. They agreed to do away with this Drechsler because they could not wait until Germany judged him. Stengel said, "Germany should be grateful to us for such action; for getting rid of such a bastard."

He confirmed that his confession was correct and in his own handwriting, but he objected to the word "premeditation" because he contended that he did not have time to think things over clearly. He challenged proof that he was there when preparations were made in the shower room to hang Drechsler. Premeditation may have applied to the other participants, but he claimed that he came by accident upon these men and only helped them because they seemed to need another man. Stengel added that if he had planned this thing and had thought it out, he certainly would not have joined this group of men without wearing gloves. Baldwin then read him the complete testimony of Alfred Friedrich, who said that Stengel had not worn gloves. Stengel denied that he had spoken to Friedrich at the football field. However, now he understood why the board was able to make a charge. After the murder, Friedrich informed him that fingerprints had been found on Drechsler's neck.

Stengel said, "Those are my fingerprints, because I wore no gloves." He bitterly asserted that Friedrich had promised never to mention his name but now he saw that Friedrich had mentioned him many times.

The next day, Baldwin drove to Hammond General Hospital in Modesto to talk to Rolf Wizuy. He followed the same procedures as with Stengel. Wizuy learned that his fellow countrymen had betrayed him when he heard the statements of Hox, Weimer and Polowzyk. He was confused as to whether he should make his statements under oath. Baldwin gave him a vague explanation of the procedure, saying that as far as he was concerned, it was immaterial whether he make it under oath or without oath.

Wizuy opted not to make his statement under oath and said that he knew that Drechsler was a traitor "one hundred percent." When Hox did not tell them what to do, Wizuy said they were led by their superiors to believe that they were to take matters into their own hands. Fischer acquired the rope with which the deceased was hanged and stifled Drechsler's cries for help by sticking his finger into his mouth. His biggest fear was being sent to an interrogation camp where they would be hanged on the word of someone like Drechsler. Wizuy believed that if the American military assumed the right to deceive them in an interrogation camp, then it automatically had an obligation to tell them that these statements were not right. Wizuy said that if it were known that all prisoners of war, whether they were good Germans or traitors, would be sent back to Germany after the war, Drechsler would still be alive. Then they would have given Drechsler a thorough beating so that he couldn't sit on his rear end for five days, but they would never have hanged him. Baldwin gave Wizuy time to think over his statement. Wizuy added that although he personally knew that Drechsler was a traitor, he was not the instigator of the crime.

Baldwin drove to the Turlock Rehabilitation Center, where he interviewed Guenther Kuelsen, who was brought up for interrogation after dinner. Kuelsen said that he was going to tell the truth and was willing to take the oath. While he had not actually carried Drechsler to the shower room, Kuelsen did give "them a hand in order to put Drechsler's head through the noose."

He then asked for time to think about what else he might want to say, and Baldwin adjourned the meeting for five minutes. Kuelsen stated that Drechsler had given an oath of allegiance to the German flag and had broken that oath. Kuelsen had difficulty understanding how Americans could punish him for the murder of a German soldier when he expected to face German authorities after the war. Baldwin replied that under the Geneva Convention Article 45, Kuelsen was subject to all the laws of the detaining power. Kuelsen understood that it would be different if he had harmed an American soldier. He did not realize that it was futile to argue his case with Baldwin, who informed him that as a prisoner of war, captured by the American forces, his conduct was covered by the 92nd Article of War, which prohibits murder. Kuelsen did not understand how he could be under American laws when he was a soldier. He had heard there were rumors that the American officers of Camp Papago Park, who conducted the first investigation, only wanted the names of the men who had participated in the crime in order to have proof to report to Germany through Red Cross channels. A frightened, bewildered Guenther Kuelsen returned to his cell.

The next morning, July 5, Baldwin went over Helmut Fischer's testimony. After Fischer heard the statement of Franz Hox, he shrugged his shoulders. He justified his actions as an act of war and declined to make a statement under oath. He said that Drechsler was a traitor who had no right to live among German soldiers. He insisted that American authorities would have to take part of the blame because they sent him to Camp Papago Park even though they knew he was a traitor. Fischer took part in hanging Drechsler because he felt that he had to act as a German soldier. He concluded with, "I have nothing more to say in my defense."

Franke had very little to say to Baldwin except for coldly acknowledging his confession. He and Wizuy tried to get a noncommissioned officer to help them give Drechsler the Holy Ghost, but Hox, Reinl, Elser, Murza and Captain Guggenberger wanted no part of it. Franke tied the dog leash around Drechsler's throat to keep him from screaming.

Bernhard Reyak described Drechsler's wild screaming when they removed him from the barracks. When an American guard jeep drove past, they dropped Drechsler and fled. A few minutes later, they were joined by Otto Stengel, and they decided that the beating Drechsler had gotten so far was insufficient. Reyak wanted to withdraw, but Stengel encouraged him to go on with it. Reyak gave a complete description of the hanging and admitted that he had taken part in the beating but insisted that he never put on his gloves because he never participated in the crime. He did admit to preparing the noose in the shower room. Reyak ran outside and waited with a group of spectators while the other six POWs carried Drechsler to the shower room. Someone came out and said, "The matter is finished." Reyak asked to see the testimony of all the witnesses who claimed that he had been present when Drechsler's head was put through the noose, but he still insisted that he was not present at the hanging. Reyak claimed that he carried the gloves inside his shirt but did not have time to put them on and that he never participated in the actual hanging. He also divulged that Reinl had told them to be careful because of fingerprints. Reyak stared at Baldwin as if wanting some sort of understanding, but none was forthcoming. He went through a lengthy justification, which he summarized with the words, "We had to prevent him from doing further harm."

Baldwin drove to Auburn, California, to interview the last defendant, Heinrich Ludwig, at DeWitt General Hospital. After dinner, Ludwig was brought in to face Baldwin, and he chose to make his statement under oath. He had roomed with Drechsler in an interrogation camp near Washington, D.C., for about ten days. Drechsler questioned him concerning secret matters regarding his submarine, and whatever Ludwig told him he later learned was repeated to the American authorities. Ludwig had also been interrogated at Fort Meade by a British officer, and every time he returned from an interrogation, a few minutes later Drechsler would be called out of the room. Ludwig said he told him several times that when he was called away, the officers questioned him as to what he had told him about the interrogation conducted by that English officer. The time interval between Ludwig's interrogation and when Drechsler was called out was about five minutes. He recalled that Drechsler had introduced himself as an officer. After confirming Ludwig's statement's correctness, Baldwin completed his investigation.

When confronted with the evidence, each man confessed but insisted that he had punished a traitor, not committed a murder. On June 30, the board, consisting of Colonel Gerald L. Church, president; Major Francis P. Walsh, recorder; and Major Herman J. Zabel reported that German prisoner of war Werner Drechsler, ISN-50-51-NA, came to his death by strangulation on the night of Sunday, March 12, 1944, at 9:30 p.m. at Camp Papago Park, Phoenix, Arizona; and that he had been murdered by hanging by German prisoners of war Otto Stengel, Rolf Wizuy, Heinrich Ludwig, Helmut Fischer, Fritz Franke, Bernhard Reyak and Guenther Kuelsen. Also, German prisoners of war Sigfried Elser and Friedrich Murza aided and assisted, counseled and advised the murderers of Drechsler prior to the murder and, in the opinion of the board, should be charged and tried as accessories before the fact. The board recommended that these prisoners be charged and tried for the murder of Werner Drechsler under the provisions of Article of War 92.

On July 11, 1944, the Ninth Service Command, Fort Douglas, Utah, issued an order signed by Colonel John H. Wilson, chief of staff, convening a court-martial for these prisoners. They would be tried as a group because they had jointly, with common intent, with malice aforethought and with premeditation, killed Werner Drechsler. The Switzerland legation in Washington, D.C., was informed via the Red Cross of the impending trial but chose not to provide a representative. The legation had received letters from POWs Friedrich Murza and Gunther Kuelsen, complaining that they were being held in solitary confinement at Camp Florence and being mistreated and not accorded the freedom to which they were entitled under the provisions of the Geneva Convention. The legation asked that the Department of State investigate the status of all prisoners held in connection with the Drechsler case.

The court-martial convened at Camp Florence on August 15 at 9:08 a.m. with Colonel Cassius Poust appointed president or judge of the court. Poust, from Sycamore, Illinois, was an able jurist with an extensive background in both civil and criminal law. The other twelve officers were a diverse and well-educated lot. Colonel Clayton J. Herman, representing the infantry, graduated from Genesee Wesleyan in New York and did postgraduate work at the University of Rochester. Herman received several decorations during both World Wars I and II. Colonel Bertram I. Lawrence, also representing the infantry, graduated from Central College in Fayette, Missouri, and did postgraduate work at University of Missouri. Colonel Callie H. Palmer represented the U.S. cavalry. The cavalry was used primarily for transportation of troops, artillery and materiel during World War II. During the period between the two world wars, the United States got rid of most of the horses and converted to a mechanized cavalry. The national horse stocks were reduced from twenty-five million in 1920 to fourteen million in 1940. The cavalry was absorbed into the army in 1950. Palmer served in the military from 1916 to 1946. Colonel Joseph H. Whiteley of the Medical Corps was decorated in both World Wars I and II. He received a degree in pharmacy from Drake in Des Moines and did postgraduate work at the University of Illinois. Colonel William H. Wertz was a member of the U.S. Army Coast Artillery Corps, which was responsible for coastal, harbor and antiaircraft defense of the United States from 1901 until 1950. Army major Robert R. Taylor graduated from college and served at the Camp Florence, Arizona POW camp. He received the Legion of Merit American Campaign Medal and the World War II Victory Medal. Major Curtis H. Wienker, of the infantry, graduated from the University of Washington. Captain James C. Reilly represented the U.S. Army Quartermaster Corps, a sustainment branch of the U.S. Army. It supports the development, production, acquisition and sustainment of general supply, mortuary affairs, subsistence, petroleum, water and distribution management during peace and war to provide combat power to the army. Reilly received several World War II decorations and attended the University of Texas at San Antonio. Captain Norman W. Edward was of the U.S. Army Ordnance Corps, whose mission was to supply army combat units with weapons and ammunition, including their procurement and maintenance. Captain Ross J. Thomas represented the Quartermaster Corps and Captain Clarence Evans the Military Police. Captain Thomas H. Carrick represented the Chemical Corps, a branch of the army assigned with defending the country against chemical, biological, radiological and nuclear attacks. The corps was founded as the U.S. Chemical Warfare Service during World War I. Carrick received a degree in chemistry from the University of California at Los Angeles. Walsh was assisted by Captain Robert O. Hillis, who had served with him on the staff of the Judge Advocate General's Office. Hillis received a law degree from the University of Indiana at Bloomington. Major William J. Taylor, an officer from the Judge Advocate Office, was appointed as defense counsel and was assisted by Major Harold A. Furst. Furst received a pharmacy degree from Drake University and a law degree from UCLA. Captain Oscar S. Schmidt, the official court interpreter, translated German to English. Private Erwin J. Gruenebaum translated the proceedings of the trial from English to German for the accused.

All seven of the accused were ordered to stand and asked individually if they wished to have Taylor and Furst as counsel. It was explained to them that personal knowledge of the counsel was not necessary. The group then

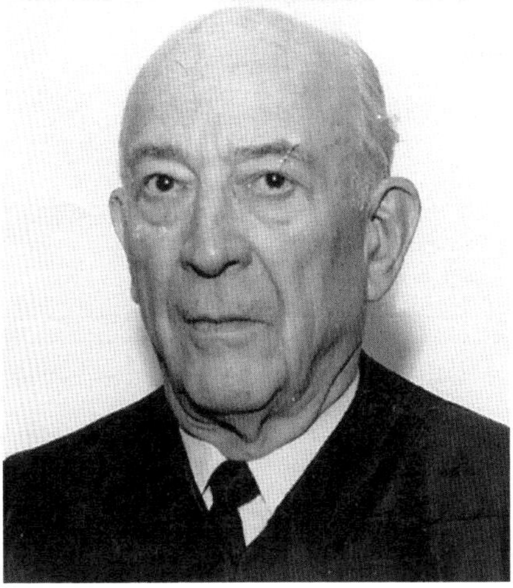

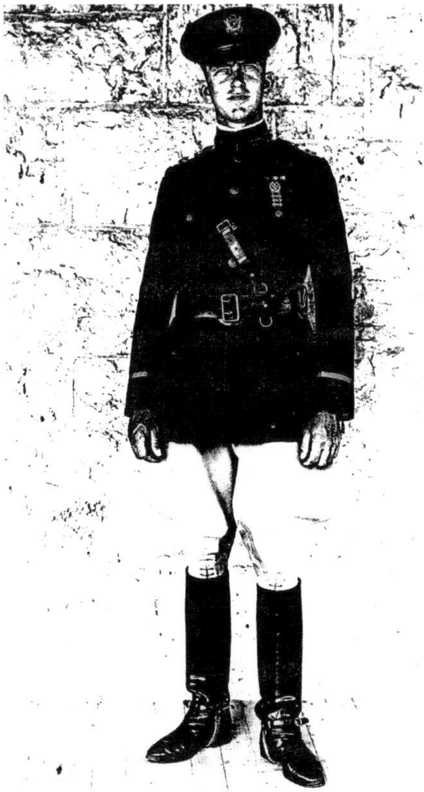

Above: Colonel Cassius Poust from Sycamore, Illinois, was an able jurist with an extensive background in both civil and criminal law. *Courtesy Sycamore, Illinois Historical Society.*

Right: Colonel Callie H. Palmer represented the U.S. cavalry on the court-martial. *Courtesy National Archives Personnel Records, St. Louis, Missouri.*

accepted Furst and Taylor. Each prisoner indicated that the court-appointed counsel would be satisfactory. Walsh read the charges, and Gruenebaum translated them into German.

Walsh asked, "Do you desire to challenge any member of the court peremptorily?" Then he told Gruenebaum to explain carefully that for this challenge they must make it as a group and were allowed only one challenge collectively. They did not understand what it meant to challenge a panel member, and so they accepted the panel. When the interpreter finished, Helmut Fischer was ordered to stand.

Walsh asked him directly if he understood the word "challenge." Fischer replied, "I do not know any of the members of the court and therefore I have nothing to say against them."

Poust explained that personal acquaintance was irrelevant and asked again if he wished to challenge. Fischer replied that he did not. The question was then put to all the defendants, who indicated that they did not wish to challenge the court. Poust swore all persons present in the court to secrecy.

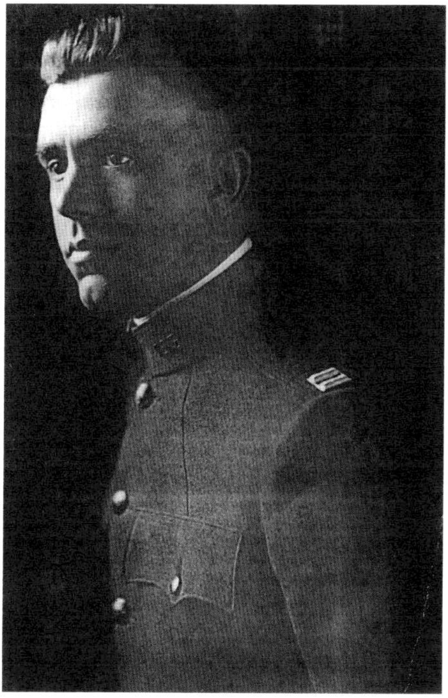

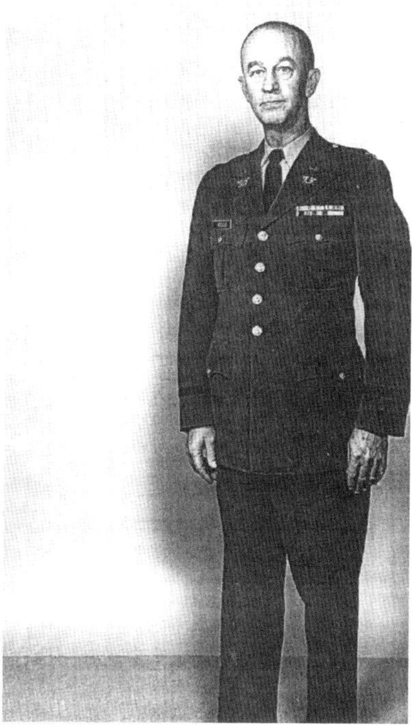

Left: Colonel Joseph H. Whiteley saw action and was decorated in both World War I and II as a member of the Medical Corps. *Courtesy National Archives Personnel Records, St. Louis, Missouri.*

Right: Captain Robert O. Hillis, who had served on the staff of the Judge Advocate General's Office of the Ninth Service Command, received a law degree from the University of Indiana. *Courtesy National Archives Personnel Records, St. Louis, Missouri.*

With the preliminaries complete, the trial began. Walsh faced the seven defendants and said, "Prisoners of war Helmut Fischer, Fritz Franke, Guenther Kuelsen, Heinrich Ludwig, Bernhard Reyak, Otto Stengel, Rolf Wizuy, I will now read the charge and specification under which you are about to be tried." Schmidt translated for the prisoners. Walsh asked each prisoner how he pleaded to the specification of murder in the first degree. Each man answered "not guilty."

Lieutenant Thomas V. Jackson, the assistant post engineer at Camp Papago Park, exhibited drawings of the prisoner of war camp, including the shower room where Drechsler was hanged. After his testimony, the court recessed, and the accused waited and smoked in the hall until Schmidt told them to put out their cigarettes. The second witness for the prosecution was Captain Cecil Parshall, who had served as commanding officer for approximately two months after the Drechsler hanging. Parshall described the condition of the body and identified the rope used in the hanging. After an examination of the body, he had posted a guard. When he described a pool of blood about two feet in diameter in the middle of the aisle near Drechsler's cot, the defense tried to establish that Parshall could not positively tell whose blood was on the floor of the barracks, nor could he identify the rope as the one used to hang Drechsler.

Captain Leland Hebblewaithe, Camp Papago Park's classification and identification officer, testified that he had obtained the minimum three fingerprints because rigor mortis set in quickly after the violent struggle. These prints matched Drechsler's personnel records. He photographed Drechsler before he and Bornstein cut down the body. Taylor asked Hebblewaithe what prior information he had of Drechsler. At first, the captain insisted that his knowledge was limited to the usual Form 2 assigning the prisoners to the camp, but under intense questioning, he admitted that he had heard that Drechsler had aided the United States. Walsh objected strenuously to Taylor's questioning as incompetent, irrelevant and immaterial, and Poust sustained the objection. It was a discovery that the Camp Papago Park officers knew about Drechsler's special status. Sergeant Fred R. Bornstein had been in charge of the ambulance detail that picked up Drechsler and two other prisoners requiring medical attention when they arrived in Arizona. Bornstein testified about Drechsler's good English and how he had helped cut down and transport Drechsler's body to the Phoenix mortuary. Captain Claude C. Stafford performed an autopsy on Drechsler late in the afternoon on March 13. Stafford, a surgeon at Pismo Beach, California, served as chief of surgery at Camp Papago Park. Captain Max Marks, who assisted Stafford and who had examined Drechsler's corpse while it was still hanging from the rafter, corroborated Stafford's findings. Stafford's autopsy described Drechsler's corpse:

> *Well developed and well nourished white young male. His face is covered with blood. His tongue is markedly swollen, and the anterior portion protrudes from the mouth. There are multiple bruises throughout his face and nose. His nose is fractured. There are multiple bruises on his back and right upper thorax. Ante-mortem skin burns completely encircle his neck in three well marked rings. There are lacerations of fingers, left hand, dirt is ground into lacerations. There are bruises on his scrotum. Multiple knotty swellings on both legs below the knees, indicating severe ante-mortem blows. Post-mortem pendant blueness on both legs and feet. No gross evidence*

of fracture, except on the nose. Muscles are large and well developed.... Diagnosis: 1. Strangulation 2. Bruises, multiple, Generalized 3. Fracture, simple, complete.

After a recess, Church, Zabel and Walsh testified. This case depended not on whether the confessions were true or false but whether they were voluntary. Taylor based much of his defense on the methods employed to get these confessions. The procedure for obtaining a conviction appeared to be legal. The defendants had been informed of their rights, confessed and returned to their cells with paper, pen and ink to write out their confessions. The 1929 Geneva Convention dictated that a prisoner did not have to answer any questions but anything he said could be held against him in a court of law. Each prisoner had signed a statement that his confession was voluntary and that no coercion had been used to obtain the confession.

Taylor asked Church whether coercion or violence had ever been used. Church replied, "Not within my presence."

"Do you have any information as to the use of coercion outside of your presence?"

Church testified that he had some information, which Taylor asked that he reveal to the court. Church admitted that Otto Stengel had been interrogated at length by persons other than the board. Taylor questioned Church about the methods used to obtain the confessions. Church said he could not answer of his own knowledge but that something had occurred to him and asked if he could tell it to the court. Poust replied that Church could tell anything he knew of his own knowledge but that he wanted nothing of hearsay or rumor. Church said that during the first part of May 1944, three of the accused had failed lie detector tests in his presence. Major Herman J. Zabel identified each of the defendants by name before the court recessed, and the prisoners returned to their cells, where they received their supper.

The court reconvened at seven o'clock that evening. Zabel testified that he added the "free, voluntary, and without coercion" phrase to each confession. He had authored the statement, translated it into German and gave it to each man. Sergeant Carl F. Blank testified as to the authenticity of the statements.

Walsh addressed the court, stating that one more witness was flying into Phoenix but would not arrive for at least two hours. The court adjourned and reconvened the next morning. By now the defendants, under heavy guard, felt certain that they would be found guilty. It had been a hot, sweltering day in Florence, and the lack of cooling in the barracks on the night of August 15 offered little chance of sleep. On August 16, they awoke at 5:30 a.m. and dressed. A half hour later, they ate breakfast in their cells. At 8:00 a.m., Major Pickard arrived with a guard to escort them to the courtroom. Lieutenant Harry Baldwin had arrived from Fort Douglas. Poust called the court to order at 8:30 a.m. and swore Baldwin in. Walsh questioned Baldwin, who identified Helmut Fischer as one of the men whom he had investigated. Baldwin's testimony was repeated with each of the other defendants. Then Taylor asked if Guenther Kuelsen had desired to make an additional statement as to why he participated in the crime. Kuelsen made an emotional statement: "One only can judge the situation I am in when one has lived through the sinking of a submarine as I have, and when one has further realized how much damage a man like Drechsler has done. I wanted to help my buddies [that] Drechsler had harmed in the past, and I wanted to prevent Drechsler from rendering further services to the Americans."[51]

In an unusual move, Taylor called Walsh to the witness stand, and he testified that he had served the charges on the seven defendants. Acknowledgements by each prisoner that he had been advised of his rights were entered as evidence.

After lunch, Taylor called Sergeant Paul Held to the witness stand. The witness would only say that his name was Paul Held, although this is now known to be an alias. He refused to reveal his organization, claiming that he was sworn to secrecy by order of the War Department. Held admitted that he had served as an interpreter when he interrogated Otto Stengel. Poust intervened and told Taylor to ask if Schmidt did any interrogation and then to inquire into his manner of questioning. Held's reply was, "Yes sir." Held continued to be uncooperative, and neither the defense nor the court-martial board could force him to reveal anything he considered as classified. Held admitted that Stengel had worn an overcoat during his interrogation but denied that any third-degree methods were used in his presence. Held told the court that Schmidt had interrogated Fritz Franke and Rolf Wizuy but denied using any special methods of interrogation and refused to disclose the location of the interrogation.

Taylor asked, "In the interrogations at which you were present, when Captain Schmidt conducted the questioning of prisoners of war Franke and Fischer, were the prisoners of war advised of their rights under the Articles of War?"

Held admitted, "Not in the beginning, sir."

Captain Oscar Schmidt was called next as a witness. When Taylor said, "State your name, rank, organization and station," Schmidt replied, "Oscar S. Schmidt, captain, Air Corps, unit is secret." His name was also an alias. He was able to identify all of the prisoners except Ludwig.

Taylor asked, "Do you recall an interrogation of Otto Stengel?" Schmidt recalled interrogating him but couldn't state the date or time.

"Did you see him, during an interrogation by yourself, dressed in an army overcoat?" When Schmidt refused to answer the question, Poust insisted that he answer.

He said, "I don't remember seeing him with an overcoat on."

"Did you use any forceful means or third-degree methods in any way or in any form?"

Schmidt asked, "What constitutes third-degree methods?"

Poust was irritated by Schmidt's arrogance, but he appeared helpless to do anything about it except to insist, "Answer yes or no."

"I used ordinary interrogation methods."

Taylor asked, "What are ordinary interrogation methods?"

"I am not allowed to divulge those methods." Poust then insisted that Taylor ask him leading questions, and Taylor forced Schmidt to admit that he had crammed an onion down a gas mask worn by Otto Stengel.

Poust ordered the seven accused to stand. He addressed them, saying that they had three choices. Each of the accused could remain silent, make an unsworn statement or testify as a witness. If they chose to remain silent, the court could not indulge in any speculation from a failure to take the stand in their own defense, and no presumption of their guilt or innocence should arise from their failure to testify. Schmidt was ordered to serve as translator. Otto Stengel chose to make an unsworn statement. He identified Schmidt and told of being taken on a ride of four hours at a high rate of speed, during which a steel rod inside the car whipped back and forth. When Schmidt asked, "Will you confess now?" Stengel said that he had nothing to confess, and the wild ride continued until they arrived back at camp. Later, he was taken on another trip where the steel rod whipped even harder and where food was withheld. He claimed to have been so exhausted that he could not walk. He was forced to wear three heavy coats and the steam heat was turned on. "My shirt and underwear were torn and my sex organs were hanging out, at which time I was pushed against the steam heat and burned myself."

Schmidt yelled, "Will you confess now or will we give you some more of Dachau treatment?" When Stengel refused, Schmidt put the gas mask over his face and rammed an onion in the air vents.

He said, "Now you see how it is if slowly the air gets out. That is the way you did it to Drechsler." When Stengel regained consciousness, he was asked, "Do you want any more of that stuff?"

Stengel said, "It is enough for me. I want to talk to the major [Church]." Stengel testified that a doctor gave him a shot that paralyzed him for three days. The doctor had denied this but said he had given a prisoner a shot for syphilis. General Clayton Russell, who oversaw the interrogations, denied that any coercion was used on the prisoners. He testified that the only instance of a prisoner being denied food was when the interrogation lasted through the regular meal time, and then the interrogating officer also went without food. He did admit that one interrogator used a gas mask on which an onion had been rubbed for a period of less than five minutes.

Helmut Fischer, who spoke very good English, told his interrogators that Schmidt had ordered him to stand at attention for several hours. When Schmidt was dissatisfied with the way he stood, he made him cross his arms under the seat of his pants. Held then stepped on his hands while yelling at him. "At first I was asked if I could remember what happened on the 12th and 13th of March. Then Capt. Schmidt asked me if I knew the pig dog Hox. At the same time he asked me if I knew something about a super Nazi, Wattenberg. I answered that I knew only a captain at sea, Wattenberg, and a Chief Quartermaster Hox. Further I was asked if I knew Dachau. I said no to the question, and then Capt. Schmidt asked me if he should show me something about Dachau. I said, 'No.' Held asked if my undershirt and my shorts were bothering me. If they did, I should denude [*sic*] myself."

Wizuy stated that he, too, had been interrogated by Schmidt and that he was held in a dark cell until he was ready to confess. When he refused to confess, he was taken on a harrowing ride through the desert for about four hours. Then he was ordered to stand at attention for several hours. Schmidt kicked him in the knees to "see if he really stood at attention" and then ridiculed him for being a superman. Wizuy was allowed to sit down, but his guards refused to let him sleep. Insisting that his circumstances would not change until he confessed, Schmidt stood behind him and pressed his shoulder blades together. Wizuy noted that Schmidt had been drinking and his eyes were bloodshot.

After the court heard the unsworn statements, Taylor announced, "The defense rests."

The prosecution waived opening arguments. Taylor stepped forward to present his arguments for the accused. At no time did he deny that the men committed the murders, but he admonished the court to be unbiased even though the country was at war with Germany and to put aside any personal animosity. He reminded the court that it may not consider the confession of an accused as evidence unless there be in the record other evidence, either direct or circumstantial, that the offense charges had been committed. There had to be evidence of the *corpus delicti* other than the confession itself. A crime had to be proven to have occurred before a person could be convicted of committing that crime. Taylor insisted that the confessions by the accused in this case had been induced by fear of punishment.

Taylor pointed out that Schmidt admitted that during Stengel's interrogation, he had used an unauthorized torture method when he placed an onion inside a gas mask before putting a mask on Stengel and closing off his air supply. Mitigating circumstances were that the accused considered themselves to be soldiers, bitter just as American soldiers would have been in discovering a traitor in their midst. They did their duty as they saw it. In closing, he asked the court to make a fair judgment. If the court found the seven men guilty of murder, then they should take into consideration the unusual circumstances surrounding the crime.

Walsh counter argued that this brutal crime should not be condoned even though Drechsler had been a traitor. He insisted, "We do not condone acts which are called acts of a traitor but neither you nor anyone can condone the treatment which was received by this poor boy before he was hung [*sic*]."

Moreover, Otto Stengel, who complained the most of ill treatment, had volunteered his services and urged the others to commit murder after some of them had decided that a beating was enough. Walsh claimed that Stengel "should have been a novelist. He is one of the greatest story tellers I have ever heard." He argued that when a German soldier or sailor is brought into this country as a prisoner of war, he is subject to all the laws of the United States of America. "You cannot commit murder. You cannot take a person out and hang him."

CHAPTER 5
CONVICTION AND APPEALS

With these statements, the court closed and the court-martial officers met in private to decide their verdict. Each of the seven defendants—Helmut Fischer, Fritz Franke, Guenther Kuelsen, Heinrich Ludwig, Bernhard Reyak, Otto Stengel and Rolf Wizuy—was found guilty as charged and sentenced "to be hanged by the neck until dead."

Poust reopened the court and informed the members that the findings and sentences would not be announced. On August 16, 1944, the trial officially closed. Although the defendants had not heard the verdict or the sentencing, they more than likely knew that they had lost. It now remained for the case to go before the board of review.

After the court-martial, Walsh remained in Phoenix for several weeks to help the court stenographer assemble the record. The imposition of the death penalty automatically opened up the channels of appeal. First, an official review by the military examined the legality of the case. The army then transmitted these findings and recommendations via the Judge Advocate General Office to Washington for approval by Secretary of War Henry Stimson and President Harry S Truman.

Henry Lewis Stimson, who served as secretary of war during both World War I and World War II, had serious misgivings about the conduct of the trial from the beginning. The military review board found no errors, omissions or irregularities that might injuriously affect the rights of the accused. The board described the court-martial record as "refreshingly free of procedural errors." However, its members noted that prosecutor Walsh improperly

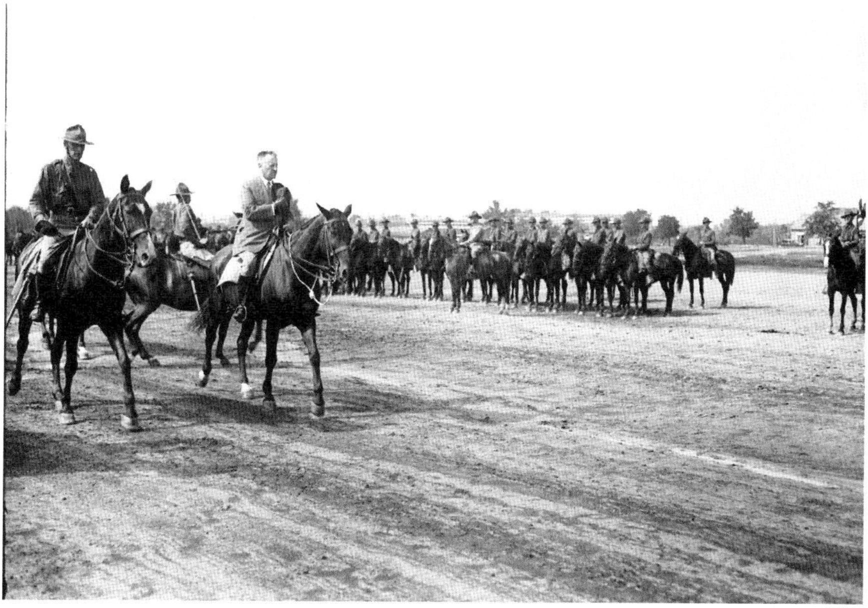

Secretary of War Henry Stimson, who served as secretary of war during both world wars, reviews the troops. *Courtesy Library of Congress.*

commented when he accused Stengel of being the motivating force in the crime and when he ridiculed the unsworn statements by the prisoners.

The court-martial record was submitted to General William Shedd, commanding general of the Ninth Service Command, who reviewed and approved the proceedings on September 15, 1944, but recommended that the sentence of each of the accused be commuted to life imprisonment. He then forwarded the record of the trial to the Judge Advocate Review Board for action. This three-man board included Colonel Terry A. Lyon, a judge advocate, and two officers from the Judge Advocate General Corps: Major Hermann Moyse and Colonel William Hepburn. Later, Colonel William Rounds joined the board, which met in November 1944 at Fort Douglas, Utah, and by February, they had completed their review. They ruled that the military had complied with the applicable articles of the Geneva Convention and that the rights of the seven accused had been scrupulously preserved. A letter had been sent to the legation of Switzerland on July 15, advising the protectorate of German rights. Colonel Archibald King of the Judge Advocate General Office ruled that the prisoners' confessions were voluntary, and in his opinion, the accused did not deserve leniency. Lyon noted that no evidence had been presented in contradiction of the POWs' participation in the hanging. Nevertheless, both he and Hepburn recommended commutation to life imprisonment. Lyon agreed that the Drechsler murder was a horrible crime, but in view of the youth of the accused, the Nazi philosophy under which they had been educated, the war hysteria and the dubious validity of their confessions, their sentences should be commuted to life imprisonment. Major Moyse and Colonel Rounds favored hanging. Rounds favored hanging because Nazi prisoners had taken the law into their own hands. He felt that commutation to life would condone the crime of murder and be viewed by prisoners as an indirect approval of their patriotism. The review board discussed the question of coercion in connection with the confessions. While no objection had been made by the accused as to the introduction of their respective confessions, the voluntary nature of the confessions was questioned at least inferentially in the testimony by the defense and in the unsworn statements by three of the accused. Lyons felt that insinuation of improper pressure merited but did require consideration. The board concluded that all seven of the accused, with clear defined malice, deliberately joined in the perpetration of a heartless, cold-blooded, premeditated murder. They had acted as judges, court and executioners in concluding that Drechsler cooperated with the United States as a traitor. The review board denied that the accused were motivated by patriotism to commit a deliberate murder. It assumed that the United States would subject itself to criticism if it took the position that prisoners of war might with impunity do violence to other prisoners because of real or fancied wrong. As for the confessions, the board of review noted that there had been ample opportunity for the accused to repudiate their confessions and they never did so. On November 17, 1944, the board of review approved the court-martial and made no recommendation for clemency.

The final review was made by Myron Cramer as head of the Judge Advocate General Department. Born in Portland, Connecticut, on November 6, 1881, Cramer graduated from Wesleyan University in 1904 and Harvard Law School in 1907. He joined the military and was promoted to first lieutenant in 1915. He served on the Mexican border with General "Black Jack" Pershing until February 1917. The judge advocate general offered Cramer a commission as major, and he was selected to be the army's top lawyer in 1941. The Drechsler case was not his first as a judge of a trial where German POWs faced the death penalty.

Cramer had worked with U.S. attorney general Francis Biddle on a trial of German U-boat saboteurs. In June 1942, eight German agents

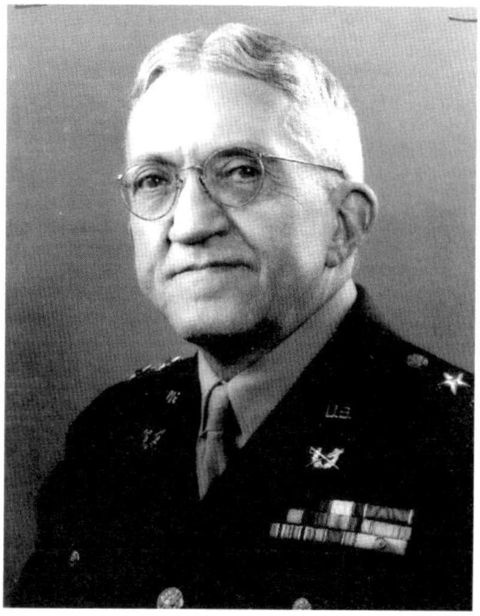

Myron Cady Cramer graduated from Harvard Law School in 1907 and served on the Mexican border with General "Black Jack" Pershing until February 1917. *Courtesy Fred Borch, Judge Advocate Office.*

traveled across the Atlantic. Four landed on Long Island, New York, and four in Florida. The saboteurs brought with them dynamite, fuses and $180,000 cash. Their instructions showed the locations of U.S. aluminum and magnesium production facilities, electric power plants and other infrastructure important to America's war effort. One of their leaders, George Dasch, turned himself in to the Federal Bureau of Investigation, and as a result, the FBI quickly apprehended the other men. Because the United States did not want Hitler to know how easy it had been for Germans to land on U.S. shores, Secretary of War Stimson and Biddle decided that a military commission closed to the public was the best course of action. The fact that Germany had secretly landed its agents in civilian guise on United States soil was an act of war. Cramer informed Stimson that a civilian court was the wrong forum for the German saboteurs because the maximum punishment would be less than desirable to impose. Under a military trial, there was no limitation on any sentence, including the death penalty. President Roosevelt established the military commission by proclamation on July 2, 1942, and issued an executive order appointing Biddle and Cramer as co-prosecutors. The military commission found all eight defendants guilty of "attempting to commit sabotage, espionage, and other hostile acts" and conspiracy to commit these same offenses. Cramer and Biddle argued for the death sentence, which Roosevelt approved for six of the eight men, and they were executed on August 8, 1942. The other two were imprisoned and deported to Germany after the war.[52]

Cramer continued to serve as the top army lawyer and made the deciding opinion on the appeals of the seven POWs who had hanged Drechsler. The army transferred them to the United States Disciplinary Barracks at Fort Leavenworth to await presidential confirmation of their death sentences. On January 27, guards handcuffed the Camp Papago Park prisoners and led them under heavy guard from the Florence guardhouse to a train destined for Fort Leavenworth, Kansas. During the entire ride, the blinds were closed.

From a high bluff, the United States Disciplinary Barracks overlooks the Missouri River at the north end of Fort Leavenworth. The prison, surrounded by massive stone walls with gun towers and a central detention building, is distinctive in that all inmates and guards are members of the military service. The normal dangers and hardships of the frontier post in Indian Territory along with the ravages of malaria resulted in a Soldiers' Burial Ground. In 1861, bodies from this cemetery were disinterred and moved to the new Fort Leavenworth National Cemetery. The first prisoner to die in confinement was John P. Hunter, who died from malaria fever on September 28, 1875. By 1883, sixteen more prisoners had died and were interred in the National Cemetery. Burying convicts in a national military cemetery is in violation of the regulations governing National Cemetery interments, so a cemetery for the U.S. military post was established in 1883 for convicts. The first prisoner to be interred in this cemetery was Sidney Williams, who died of pneumonia on March 10, 1884. The military prison utilized this new cemetery for twenty-six interments from 1884 until the prison was turned over to the newly founded Federal Prison Department in 1895. In 1915, the name was changed the U.S. Disciplinary Barracks. From 1929 until 1940, the U.S. Disciplinary Barracks served as an annex to the Leavenworth Federal Penitentiary. The institution underwent major renovations to three of its four cell houses. In 2011, the Federal Bureau of Prisons proposed a new 1,500-bed medium-security and 300-bed minimum-security facility on the current prison grounds. The U.S. Disciplinary Barracks Cemetery is located northwest of the main confinements facility. Regulations prescribe that only the name and date of those who die without honor will appear on the military-style headstone. What remains is a piece of paper: "Legal Execution; fracture, simple near joint with dislocation of cervical spine, severe inflicted by hanging, myocardial failure."

CHAPTER 6

EXECUTION

Colonel William Stuart Eley, the prison commandant, coped with a daily barrage of problems. A graduate of the U.S. Military Academy at West Point, his grades were average, and he was given to silly pranks from time to time. Now he faced the most difficult problem of his career. Truman had not yet signed the orders for the execution of Drechsler's murderers, and Secretary of War Henry L. Stimson was deeply concerned about the legality of the trial.

Stimson, a secretary of war in both world wars, became one of the most respected U.S. leaders. He took a strong stand against German military expansion in Europe. However, his foreign policy was tempered by a strong racial bias, as reflected by his resistance to racially integrating the armed forces and his insistence on the internment of Japanese Americans in the western United States. Concerning Drechsler's murderers, Stimson wrote, "I am very unhappy over that particular situation," and demanded answers to a set of questions within a week. Church was ordered to put nothing in writing but to report to General Archer Lerch, provost marshal general, in Washington, D.C., as soon as possible. Stimson wanted to know who participated in the methods of interrogation, what agencies they represented and the full identifications of Schmidt and Held. General B.M. "Babe" Bryan admitted that the court-martial contained "obnoxious material" that should not be forwarded to either the Swiss legation or Germany. Church flew to Washington, D.C., to personally explain the situation to Stimson.

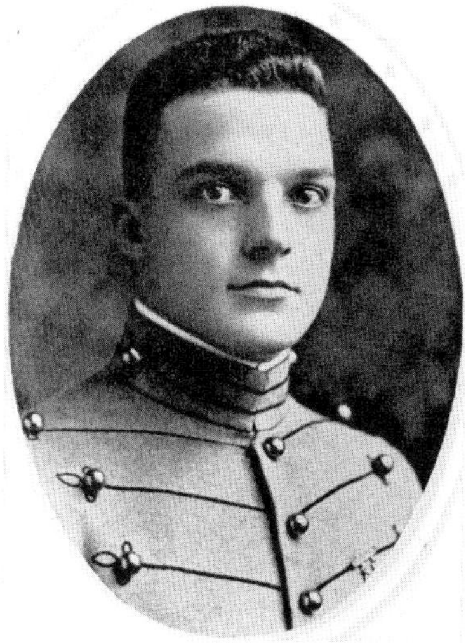

Colonel William Stuart Eley, Fort Leavenworth prison commandant, was a graduate of the U.S. Military Academy at West Point. Executing fourteen prisoners was the most difficult problem of his career. *Courtesy U.S. Military Academy at West Point.*

What was said between these men is not recorded, but after investigating the case, Stimson concurred that Drechsler's executioners should be hanged without delay. On September 21, Defense Counsel Major William H. Taylor and Assistant Defense Counsel Major Harold A. Furst informed Poust that the court-martial record might have been altered in an improper manner. In addition, members of the Judge Advocate Office voiced their opinions that Walsh had made an error in his closing argument when he ridiculed the accused who failed to take the stand and those who made only unsworn statements.

On January 5, 1945, the State Department received a note from the German legation in Switzerland stating that two Americans were being held under death sentences in Germany. The Germans requested that the Americans consider an exchange of American prisoners for the German prisoners. Stimson accused the Germans of holding Americans on trumped-up charges. He did not believe that the Germans held any American prisoners. However, the United States did not execute any Germans until all avenues of prisoner exchange negotiations had been explored.

On a dreary, damp morning, January 29, the train carrying the condemned Germans from Camp Papago Park pulled into Kansas City, Missouri. The Germans climbed into an armed truck for transport to Leavenworth, where they passed between two granite pillars and stopped before the military police booth. Through these same gates had passed many military figures of importance, including General Dwight D. Eisenhower, General John "Black Jack" Pershing and Buffalo Bill Cody. The handcuffed POWs were processed and led to their cells in the basement of a wing of the central detention building known as the "castle." Each man was assigned to a cell in the alphabetical order that they would be executed. Brick walls separated the five-foot by ten-foot cells, which had bars on the front and a concrete wall at the back. The cells of the Camp Papago Park prisoners faced the defendants in the Beyer and Gauss cases. During the day, they were allowed into the corridor and the groups could converse with each other.

During the first few days, the prisoners were interviewed by Colonel Eley, doctors, a psychiatrist and a Red Cross representative. On the second day, they met with two chaplains, Major John Sagar, Episcopalian, and Captain George Towle, Roman Catholic. Towle would minister primarily to the Camp Papago Park prisoners. Fischer, Kuelsen and Reyak had been raised as Roman Catholics while the rest were nominally Lutheran, except for Stengel, who professed the Evangelical faith. The two chaplains held out no false promises of hope but offered to be there if the Germans needed someone to talk to.

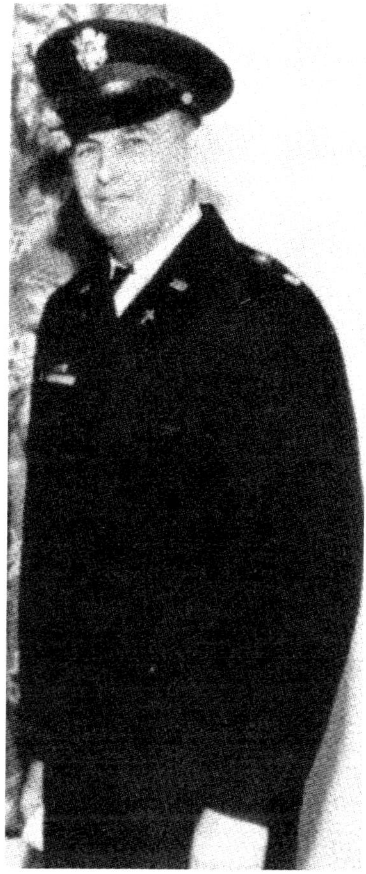

Chaplain George C. Towle counseled the prisoners from their arrival until their final execution. *Courtesy National Archives, Washington, D.C.*

Communication in Germany rapidly deteriorated. The great industrial Ruhr Valley fell into ruins. The Russians closed in the eastern front. Hitler began a purge of his closest advisers and issued an order that all military and industrial installations be destroyed before they fell into Allied hands. On April 12, the State Department received a communication from the minister of Switzerland informing the United States that the German government was prepared to exchange fifteen American prisoners of war under sentence of death for an equal number of Germans. The State Department forwarded the communication to the War Department, and on April 27, the United States asked which German POWs the German government wished to have exchanged. The legation in Switzerland acknowledged receipt of the proposal but had been unable to communicate with responsible authorities in Germany. The United States agreed to postpone any execution date. Through the Swiss, the Germans assured the United States that for the moment, the death sentences against the American prisoners of war would not be carried out. After Hitler took his life on April 30, no more attempts were made to communicate with the Germans. With the total collapse of Germany and the resignation of Switzerland as its protective power, no one remained to assist the condemned prisoners.

At Fort Leavenworth, the prisoners met daily with Chaplain Towle. They were most concerned that when the war ended, they would have to stand trial all over again in Germany. On April 13, the seven accused learned that President Franklin D. Roosevelt had died. They speculated that Roosevelt's death might be a stroke of luck for Germany. Perhaps the new president might join forces with Germany against Russia. Little did they know about Harry S Truman. On May 8, they learned of Adolf Hitler's suicide and Germany's unconditional surrender. The War Department transmitted news to the provost marshal general that the American soldiers under the death sentence by the Germans were safe and on their way home. The bargaining was over, and no legal reason remained to hold off on the executions.

In early July, Eley received orders from Stimson directing him to execute those involved in the Beyer and Gauss cases. Papers authorizing the execution of the Camp Papago Park prisoners were signed by President Truman on July 28, 1945.[53] On July 3, the unconfirmed death sentences of Edgar Menschner and Helmut Fischer, Fritz Franke, Guenther Kuelsen, Heinrich Ludwig, Bernhard Reyak, Otto Stengel and Rolf Wizuy had been forwarded to President Truman. At the same time, Truman was considering dropping atomic bombs on Hiroshima and Nagasaki. Every day, horrors of the death camps such as Dachau and Buchenwald came to the attention of the public. Pictures of cadavers stacked like so much cordwood enraged the Americans, who were in no mood to show mercy to German POWs.

Eley ordered Colonel Raymond Orr, U.S. Disciplinary Barracks quartermaster officer, to build a special set of gallows, which would have to effectively accommodate at least five and later seven consecutive hangings. On July 6, 1945, Truman commuted the sentence of Edgar Menschner for beating to death prisoner of war Hans Geller at Camp Chaffee, Arkansas. The prisoners congratulated him when guards removed him from his basement cell to begin serving a twenty-year sentence of hard labor at Fort Leavenworth. Menschner's commutation gave hope to the remaining prisoners on death row. However, at that very moment, the final touches were being put on their gallows. Now that the orders had been signed by the president, the executions would have to be carried out as quickly and humanely as possible. Eley did not want to use the central detention building as the gallows site because the 120 German and 18 Italian prisoners of war were already nervous, and he did not want to exacerbate the situation in the overcrowded prison. He selected an old quartermaster depot as the site for the executions. The structure, about 250 yards from the central detention building, served as a salvage warehouse with tailor and electric shops. Prisoners worked in the tailor shop, making the black death hoods to be worn by the condemned. Within two days, engineers erected the gallows over an elevator shaft. Eley inspected the finished product with Orr and the three civilian engineers.

At midnight on July 10, one by one, Beyer, Seidel, Demme, Scholz and Schomer were led from their cells and hanged for the murder of Johannes Kunze. Four days later, on July 14, Erich Gauss and Rudolf Straub made identical journeys for strangling a fellow prisoner, Horst Guenther.

Still on death row were the Camp Papago Park prisoners: Helmut Fischer, twenty-two; Fritz Franke, twenty-one; Guenther Kuelsen, twenty-two; Heinrich Ludwig, twenty-five; Bernhard Reyak, twenty-one; Otto Stengel, twenty-six; and Rolf Wizuy, twenty-three, convicted of the murder of Werner Drechsler. They lost all hope that their sentences might be commuted. Father George Towle helped them write letters home while begging them not to take their bitterness to their graves. At 9:25 p.m. on August 23, a guard swung open the corridor door, and Colonel Eley marched in with a guard. He read General Court Martial Order Number 406. The seven Camp Papago Park prisoners listened in stunned silence as they heard their names intoned and the charge of "Guilty" with the sentence "To be hanged by the neck until dead." Eley informed the prisoners that "the orders signed by the President of the United States and issued by the Secretary of War would be carried out on August 25, 1945, commencing at zero zero zero of that date." Eley did an abrupt about-face and left.

Chaplain Towle remained with the prisoners.[54] Otto Stengel protested bitterly, "These swines, these miserable swines. Why the hell are they doing this? They haven't understood anything after all."

Wizuy said, "It doesn't matter anymore. It's all over. It's too late now."

Kuelsen turned to Chaplain Towle and asked, "So it's going to happen tomorrow night, right?"

Towle made arrangements for them to meet their death in their uniforms, which were brought out of storage and cleaned. The next morning, the prisoners were called at 5:30 a.m., but they were already awake. They ate a breakfast of French toast, bacon, cereal, oranges and coffee. Towle arrived around 8:00 a.m. to help the condemned through the next difficult hours. The Germans had come to depend on Towle, who promised to remain with them until the end. A sense of bitterness came over the group, and they felt that they had been deserted by God and everyone. At 11:30 a.m., the men ate lunch with Towle. During the afternoon, they finished their letters and talked among themselves. For a while, the prisoners discussed religion with Towle. Tradition decreed that condemned prisoners could have whatever they wanted for their last meal. The regular meal included roast beef stew, steamed rice, creamed asparagus, a relish dish, coffee cake, bread, butter and coffee. Reyak and Wizuy did not care what they were served, but the others asked for southern fried chicken, a dish they had become very fond of while in the United States.

The Germans wore their uniforms for the first time since their capture. At 10:00 p.m., Eley ordered Father Towle to report to his office. Towle and a Protestant chaplain, Captain Wilford Garner, marched with the condemned men. Garner wore his uniform. Towle wore a black cassock and his four-cornered biretta cap, topped with a black pom. In Eley's office, several officers, along with selected reporters, waited to witness the executions. The Fort Leavenworth Public Information Office gave each witness a folder containing personal data on each prisoner, a copy of the confirmation signed by President Truman, a description of the operation of the gallows and a menu of the food served the condemned on their last day. Colonel Eley briefed the witnesses as to the procedure. The witnesses included Major Erwin S. Chappell, surgeon; Chaplain George Towle; Captain Wilfred R. Garner, Protestant chaplain; Colonel Raymond Orr; Colonel Frederick Gaumnitz; Major Louis Rosenberg; and Captain Glenn M. Bradley.

After this briefing, Towle returned to comfort the prisoners. A few minutes before midnight, the group heard approaching footsteps. A lieutenant, a sergeant, six guards with rifles and two guards with keys entered the corridor. The lieutenant announced, "Helmut Fischer." A guard unlocked Fischer's cell door. He bade farewell to his friends. After the guard put on the manacles, Fischer started his march to the brightly lit gallows room. The group marched toward the salvage warehouse. Upon entering the warehouse, the guard and Fischer stopped in front of Colonel Eley, who called everyone to attention and pronounced the sentence "to be hanged by the neck until dead." He asked Fischer if he had a last statement. Fischer remarked that he just wanted to thank Chaplain Towle. Eley said, "May God have mercy on your soul." His guard detail led Fischer onto the platform where a sergeant waited to spring the lever. Two soldiers bound Fischer's hands and feet. A third soldier pulled a black hood over his head. The room filled with an awful silence as the witnesses stared at the hooded lone figure. Eley signaled by raising his arm out to his right side and letting it drop. The sergeant plunged the lever forward, and the trapdoor sprang open. Helmut Fischer dropped into eternity. Towle went under the platform where Fischer still convulsed. He cut the hood and anointed Fischer. Three doctors certified Helmut Fischer's death.

Towle returned to the six prisoners. The guard had already formed to take Fritz Franke to his destiny. Franke said goodbye to his comrades and marched stiffly to the gallows. When Eley asked if he had any final words, he said, "No." For the second time, Eley pronounced the sentence and gave the signal to execute.

On the third trip, reporters accompanied Guenther Kuelsen. The chaplain followed behind the guard detail. Kuelsen said goodbye to his friends. His last statement contained a words of thanks for Towle. Shortly after one o'clock, Guenther Kuelsen plunged to eternity into the basement of a warehouse. The reporters chose not to go back for Heinrich Ludwig.

The four remaining men spoke little. In his last statement, Ludwig thanked the priest. At 1:30 a.m., the trapdoor sprang open, and the fall broke his neck in one clean fracture. Bernhard Reyak extinguished a cigarette before making his final journey. Although fearful and trembling, he marched resolutely to the gallows. When asked if he had any last words, Reyak said nothing. Eley repeated the question, and Reyak responded with a curt "No." The sergeant sprung the trapdoor. Only Rolf Wizuy and Otto Stengel remained.

Stengel heard his name called. He shook hands with Wizuy and asked if he might take a picture of his wife and children with him to the grave. Towle got the picture from Stengel's cell and put it in his shirt pocket. The dogwoods were in bloom. Stengel commented to Towle, "Lovely flowers, aren't they? It's been such a long time since I've seen flowers." He talked constantly and complained that his portion of chicken had been too skimpy. When Eley asked for a last statement, Stengel said, "I am fortunate that I have known the chaplain, and I think that the colonel was very correct in handling us and we received excellent treatment while we were here." The trapdoor sprung, and Stengel, at age twenty-six the oldest of the group, dropped into eternity.

When the guard came for Wizuy, he had no one to say goodbye to. Towle noticed that his body trembled. When he tried to help him get up, Wizuy said, "I'm all right." Wizuy marched unsteadily between his guards. When he faced Eley, his last statement was a word of thanks to Towle. He mumbled a prayer while a guard pulled the black hood over his face. It took eighteen minutes for him to die. When Towle anointed him, the black hood had been stripped off and his hands and feet were unbound.

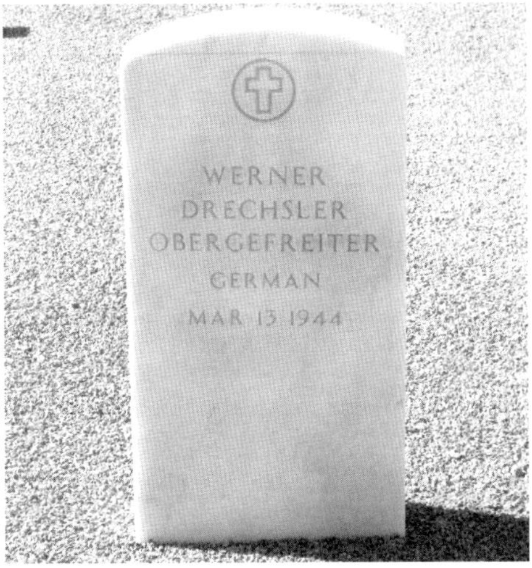

Right: Final resting place of Werner Drechsler. *Courtesy Fort Bliss military cemetery*.

Below: The burial of Drechsler's executioners along with seven others convicted of similar crimes. *Courtesy Fort Leavenworth*.

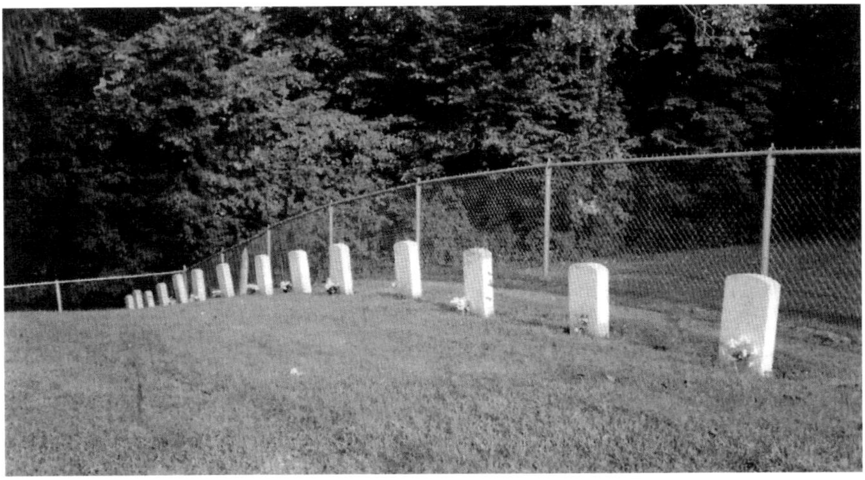

Towle worried until his death that the army blankets did not completely cover the men and their feet stuck out from under the blankets. The entire operation took about three hours. Towle chose to walk back to his quarters, where he sat in a chair at a window until the sun came up. The prisoners are buried at the U.S. Disciplinary Barracks cemetery on the Kansas prairie. Regulations decree that only name, rank and date of death—August 24 and 25, 1945—of those who die without honor will appear on the headstones. These prisoners were buried facedown, an additional mark of their dishonor. Werner Drechsler was given an American burial at Fort Bliss military cemetery in Texas.

APPENDIX A

ARTICLES OF WAR

The Fourth Geneva Convention further divides protected civilians into three categories: aliens in the territory of a party to the conflict, persons in occupied territory and internees. These three groups are provided with protections that vary according to membership in one group or another, but all must be given the basic protection codified in Article 27: respect, protection and humane treatment under all circumstances. Additional Protocol I of 1977 supplies an ingredient missing from the Fourth Convention. Specifically, Article 51 states that any civilian "enjoys general protection against dangers arising from military operations" and forbids direct attacks against them as well as so-called indiscriminate attacks, which do not distinguish between civilians and combatants. Additional Protocol I also elaborates on Fourth Convention provisions that relief actions be undertaken if a civilian population is not adequately provided with the basic supplies essential to its survival.

24TH ARTICLE OF WAR

Now Prisoner of War ______, I am going to read you the 24th Article of War. It is one of the rules governing the American Army and prisoners of war in custody of the American Army. When an enemy prisoner is captured by the American Army he is subject to the Articles of War and that one of the Articles of War is the 24th Article of War. This Article of War is entitled, "Compulsory Self-Incrimination Prohibited," and it reads as follows: No witness before a military court, commission, court of inquiry, or board, or before any officer conducting an investigation, or before any officer, military or civil, designated to take a deposition to be read as evidence before a military court, commission, court of inquiry, or board, or before an officer conducting an investigation, shall be compelled to incriminate himself or to answer any question the answer to which may tend to incriminate him, or to answer any question not material to the issue when such an answer might tend to degrade him.

Article 42

The use of weapons against prisoners of war, especially against those who are escaping or attempting to escape, shall constitute an extreme measure, which shall always be preceded by warnings appropriate to the circumstances.

Article 43

Upon the outbreak of hostilities, the Parties to the conflict shall communicate to one another the titles and ranks of all the persons mentioned in Article 4 of the present Convention, in order to ensure equality of treatment between prisoners of equivalent rank. Titles and ranks which are subsequently created shall form the subject of similar communications.

The Detaining Power shall recognize promotions in rank which have been accorded to prisoners of war and which have been duly notified by the Power on which these prisoners depend.

Article 44

Officers and prisoners of equivalent status shall be treated with the regard due to their rank and age.

In order to ensure service in officers' camps, other ranks of the same armed forces who, as far as possible, speak the same language, shall be assigned in sufficient numbers, account being taken of the rank of officers and prisoners of equivalent status. Such orderlies shall not be required to perform any other work.

Supervision of the mess by the officers themselves shall be facilitated in every way.

Article 45

Prisoners of war other than officers and prisoners of equivalent status shall be treated with the regard due to their rank and age.

Supervision of the mess by the prisoners themselves shall be facilitated in every way.

Article 66
Geneva Convention, July 27, 1929: If the death penalty is pronounced against a prisoner of war, a communication setting forth in detail the nature and circumstances of the offense shall be sent as soon as possible to the Power in whose armies the prisoner served. The sentence shall not be executed before the expiration of a period of at least three months after this communication.

Article 89
Good order to be maintained and wrongs redressed. All persons subject to military law are to behave themselves orderly in quarters, garrison, camp, and on the march; and any person subject to military law who commits any waste or spoil, or willfully destroys any property whatsoever (unless by order of his commanding officer), or commits any kind of depredation or riot, shall be punished as a court-martial may direct. Any commanding officer who, upon complaint made to him, refuses or omits to see reparation made to the party injured, in so far as the offender's pay shall go toward such reparation, as provided for in article 105, shall be dismissed from the service, or otherwise punished, as a court-martial may direct.

Article 92
A prisoner of war who attempts to escape and is recaptured before having made good his escape in the sense of Article 91 shall be liable only to a disciplinary punishment in respect of this act, even if it is a repeated offence.

A prisoner of war who is recaptured shall be handed over without delay to the competent military authority. Article 88, fourth paragraph, notwithstanding, prisoners of war punished as a result of an unsuccessful escape may be subjected to special surveillance. Such surveillance must not affect the state of their health, must be undergone in a prisoner of war camp, and must not entail the suppression of any of the safeguards granted them by the present Convention.

Article 93
Escape or attempt to escape, even if it is a repeated offence, shall not be deemed an aggravating circumstance if the prisoner of war is subjected to trial by judicial proceedings in respect of an offence committed during his escape or attempt to escape.

In conformity with the principle stated in Article 83, offences committed by prisoners of war with the sole intention of facilitating their escape and which do not entail any violence against life or limb, such as offences against public property, theft without intention of self-enrichment, the drawing up or use of false papers, or the wearing of civilian clothing, shall occasion disciplinary punishment only.

Prisoners of war who aid or abet an escape or an attempt to escape shall be liable on this count to disciplinary punishment only.

Article 94

If an escaped prisoner of war is recaptured, the Power on which he depends shall be notified thereof in the manner defined in Article 122, provided notification of his escape has been made.

APPENDIX B

CREW LIST OF THE *U-118*

Survivors

Name	Rank	U.S. Navy Equivalent	Age
Behlke, Gustaf	Matrosenobergefreiter	Seaman 1 class	21
Bort, Wilhelm	Matrosenobergefreiter	Seaman 1 class	23
Drechsler, Werner	Mechanikerobergefreiter	Seaman 1 class	23
Gross, Josef	Stabsober maschinist	Chief machinist	32
Höller, Josef	Oberfunkmaat	Radioman 1 class	24
Lenk, Erhard	Mechanikerobergefreiter	Seaman 1 class	19
Polowzyk, Herman	Matrosenobergefreiter	Fireman 2 class	21
Preuss, Klaus	Mechanikergefreiter	Seaman 2 class	19
Reinl, Werner	Oberbootsmaat	Boatswain's mate 2 class	27
Reum, Paul	Maschinengefreiter	Fireman 3 class	19
Schiller, Walter	Maschinengefreiter	Fireman 3 class	20
Siebert, Hans	Bootsmaat	Coxswain	29
Wiedemann, Herman	Maschincnmaat	Fireman 1 class	20

Name	Rank	U.S. Navy Equivalent	Age
Wiemer, Rudolf	Oberfunkmaat	Radioman 1 class	24
Wilke, Werner	Maschinenmaat	Fireman 1 class	
Wosnitzka, Hans	Matrosenobergefreiter	Seaman 1 class	22

Casualties

Name	Rank	U.S. Navy Equivalent	Age
Bassitta, Bolislaus	Matrosenobergefreiter	Seaman 1 class	21
Bohrer, Paul	Matrosenobergefreiter	Seaman 1 class	19
Borzymowski, Walther	Matrosenobergefreiter	Seaman 1 class	20
Brauer, Helmut	Maschinengefreiter	Fireman 3 class	19
Busse, Werner	Funkgefreiter	Seaman 2 class	21
Czygan, Werner	Korvettenkapitän zur See	Lieut. Commander	38
Dannenberg, ?	Oberfähnrich zur See	Midshipman	18
Dee, Theodor	Bootsmaat	Coxwain	27
Dettmer, Karl	Funkobergefreiter	Seaman 1 class	20
Doblies, Wilhelm	Matrosenobergefreiter	Seaman 1 class	29
Ervin, Wilhelm	Matrosenobergefreiter	Seaman 1 class	23
Götze, Herman	Oberleutnant (Ing.)	Lieutenant (j.g.)	24
Grass, Heinz	Maschinenobergefreiter	Fireman 2 class	20
Grauer, ?	Maschinenobergefreiter	Fireman 2 class	20
Henschel, Herbert	Sanitatsgefreiter	Medical corpsman	18
Holm, Fritz	Leutnant zur See	Ensign	29
Jaeger, Hans	Obersteuermann	Quartermaster (Warrant rank)	33
Janosch, Helmut	Maschinenobergefreiter	Fireman 2 class	22

Name	Rank	U.S. Navy Equivalent	Age
Kallenbach, Erwin	Mechanikerobermaat	Torpedoman's mate 2 class	26
Klem, Paul	Maschinenmaat	Fireman 1 class	20
Korte, Heinrich	Obermaschinist	Machinist	
Krenzin, Gunter	Maschinenmaat	Fireman 1 class	20
Kurschatke, Richard	Maschinengefreiter	Fireman 3 class	19
Minderlein, Hans	Maschinengefreiter	Fireman 3 class	19
Müller, ?	Maschinengefreiter	Fireman 3 class	19
Münch, Erhard	Maschinenobergefreiter	Fireman 2 class	22
Polster, ?	Maschinenmaat	Fireman 1 class	22
Raschke, Arno	Maschinenobergefreiter	Fireman 2 class	23
Reuter, Gunther	Leutnant (Ing.)	Ensign (Engineering duties only)	21
Richt, Helmut	Matrosengefreiter	Seaman 2 class	19
Scharfschwert, ?	Maschinengefreiter	Fireman 3 class	19
Schmidt, Heins	Maschinengefreiter	Fireman 3 class	20
Schröder, ?	Matrosenobergefreiter	Seaman 1 class	20
Schrotke, Hienrich	Oberleutnant zur See	Lieutenant (j.g.)	31
Schumann, Gerhard	Maschinenmaat	Fireman 1 class	23
Schwartz, Wilhelm	Maschinenmaat	Fireman 1 class	24
Storch, Otto	Maschinenobergefreiter	Fireman 2 class	20
Walter, ?	Oberfähnrich zur See	Midshipman	24
Winter, Bernhard	Marinestabsarzt	Lieutenant (M)	36
Wolf, Bernhard	Oberfähnrich zur See	Midshipman	19
Worch, Erich	Matrosengefreiter	Seaman 2 class	22

NOTES

Introduction

1. Eileen G. Harrison, letter to the author, October 4, 1996.
2. Moore, *Faustball Tunnel.*
3. Prange, *At Dawn We Slept.*
4. Convention relative to the Treatment of Prisoners of War, Geneva, July 27, 1929.
5. Beevor, *Berlin.*
6. Doyle, *World War II in Numbers.*
7. Weglyn, *Years of Infamy.*
8. Hamann, *On American Soil.*
9. *Chicago Tribune*, May 1943.
10. Hamann, *On American Soil.*
11. *Los Angeles Times*, June 1945.
12. Colonel William Holden file, U.S. military personnel records, St. Louis, Missouri.
13. Hamann, *On American Soil.*
14. Badoglio, *Italy in the Second World War.*

Chapter 1

15. Hemmingway, *Ira Hayes*.
16. Hamann, *On American Soil*.
17. Triangle T Ranch Records, Bureau of Land Management.
18. Interview with the late Rhea Robinson.
19. National Archives files, Special War Problems, RG 59.

Chapter 2

20. NARA letter from Anna Stengel on the wrongful death of her husband on behalf of her children and herself.
21. Mason, "U-boat Archive."
22. *Phoenix Gazette*, September 8, 1943.
23. Letter signed by General Paul B. Clemens, director of Security and Intelligence Division, March 3, 1941.
24. Verne Austin, Military Records, St. Louis, Missouri.

Chapter 3

25. Papago Trackers newsletter,
26. Personal interviews with Dorothy and Lawrence Jorgensen, December 1994–January 1995.
27. RG 389, letter from Colonel George Barber to Ninth Service Command, Fort Douglas, Utah, National Archives, May 9, 1944.
28. RG 319, IRR Box 338, Hermann Ritter.
29. *Der Ruf* or the *Call* was a propaganda sheet produced by the American military with a staff of eighty-five anti-Nazis. Court-martial vol. 3, 34.
30. RG 319 IRR Box 338, Friedrich Murza.
31. Moore, *Faustball Tunnel*, 16–21.
32. Parshall saw action with General John J. Pershing's expeditionary force in France during World War I. He was awarded the Silver Star for bravery and two Purple Hearts and several other awards. Cecil St. Claire Parshall Military Personnel Records.
33. RG 318, IRR Box 338, Oskar Meyer interrogation.
34. RG 319, IRR Box 338, Johann Neumair.
35. RG 319, IRR Box 338, Guenther Albert.

36. RG 319, IRR Box 338, Siegfried Elser.
37. General court-martial, vol. 1, vol. 2, vol. 3.

Chapter 4

38. Court-martial. Otto Stengel confession, vol 3.
39. RG 319, IRR Box 338, Guenther Bleise.
40. Court-martial vol. 3, Wizuy confession
41. Court-martial vol. 3, Ludwig confession.
42. RG 319, IRR Box 338, Werner Reinl.
43. Court-martial vol. 3, Fischer confession.
44. RG 319, IRR Box 338, Werner Reinl.
45. RG 319, IRR Box 338, Hermann Polowyzk.
46. RG 319, IRR Box 338, Lothar Mandelkow.
47. RG 319, IRR Box 338, Walter Nieswand.
48. RG 319, IRR Box 338, Johann Matzke.
49. Court-martial, Fischer et al., Lieutenant Harry Baldwin.
50. Ibid.
51. Court-martial, Fischer et al., Kuelsen.

Chapter 5

52. *Prologue* 41, no. 2 (Summer 2009).

Chapter 6

53. Execution order by Harry S Truman, Truman Library.
54. Telephone interview with the late Anna Towle.

BIBLIOGRAPHY

Primary Sources

Mason, Jerry. "U-boat Archive." www.uboatarchive.net/index.html.

National Archives. Camp Papago Park, Arizona, Administrative Files, Location Box 2483.

ONI (Office of Naval Intelligence) Special Activities Branch (OP-16-Z). Administrative Correspondence. Taylor Day Files. 1-2-43 to 5-31-45.

RG 59 Department of State Records. 1942–1944, World War II, Germans Prisoners of War.

RG 59 Records of the Board of Inquiry on the Camp Papago Park Prisoner of War Escape. Box 1373.

RG 165 National Archives. Chiefs of Staff G-2 Intelligence Division, Captured Personnel and Materials Branch, Enemy POW Interrogation File (MIS-Y). Werner Drechsler, Box 402.

RG 319 Records of the Investigative Records Repository (IRR). Box 338. These records are accessioned in increments and are security declassified at the time of accessioning.

RG 389 National Archives. Enemy Prisoner of War Information Bureau Reporting Branch, Subject File, 1942–1946.

RG 389 National Archives. Internal Security Division, Coordination Branch, Subject File, 1937–1946, Investigative Program, Subversive Program, Postwar Planning, Security Intelligence Corps and School.

RG 389 National Archives. Prisoner of War Operations Division, Legal Branch, Numeric Subject File, Operations Branch, Unclassified Decimal File and Information Bureau, Subject File.

RG 389 National Archives. Prisoner of War Special Projects Division. Administrative Branch, Decimal File, 1943–1946.

RG 389 National Archives. *U-118* Interrogation Reports, Report on the Interrogation of Survivors from *U-118* sunk on 12 June 1943. Box 1.

RG 389 Provost Marshal General Office. Report—Camp Papago Park, Box 2668.

RG 407 National Archives. Army Adjutant General Classified Decimal File, 1943–1945.

Transcript of trial of Germans Prisoners of War Helmut Fischer, Fritz Franke, Guenther Kuelsen, Heinrich Ludwig, Bernhard Reyak and Rolf Wizuy for the murder of Werner Drechsler. Ninth Service Command. U.S. Army Judiciary, Falls Church, Virginia.

Books

Adenaur, Konrad. *Memoirs, 1945–53*. Chicago: Henry Regnery Company, 1966.

Badoglio, Pietro. *Italy in the Second World War: Memories and Documents.* Westport, CT: Greenwood Press, 1948.

Beevor, Antony. *Berlin: The Downfall, 1945*. New York: Viking-Penguin Books, 2002.

Carell, Paul. *The Prisoners.* Excerpts translated from the German FRG Office of Defense Administration USA/Canada, Foreign Language Department. File No. 455/90.

Conot, Robert E. *Justice at Nuremberg*. New York: Carroll & Graf Publishers, 1983.

Cullum, George W. *Biographical Register of the Officers and Graduates of the U.S. Military Academy at West Point, New York Since Its Establishment in 1802*. Supplement vol. 6-B. 1910–1920. N.p., 1920.

Doyle, Peter. *World War II in Numbers: An Infographic Guide to the Conflict, Its Conduct, and Casualties*. Ontario, CAN: Firefly Press Richmond Hill, 2013.

Flory, William S. *Prisoners of War: A Study in the Development of International Law.* Washington, D.C.: American Council on Public Affairs, 1942.

Gansburg, Judith M. *Stalag: U.S.A.* New York: Thomas J. Crowell, 1977.

Hamann, Jack. *On American Soil: How Justice Became a Casualty of World War II.* Seattle: University of Washington Press, 2005.

Hemmingway, Al. *Ira Hayes: Pima Marine.* Lamham, MD: University Press of America, 1988.

Jaworski, Leon. *After Fifteen Years.* Houston, TX: Gulf Publishing Company, 1961.

Lamb, David. *A Sense of Place: Listening to Americans.* New York: Times Books, Random House, n.d.

Lewis, George, and John Mewha. *History of Prisoner of War Utilization by the United States Army, 1776–1945.* Washington, D.C.: Department of the Army, 1955.

Millett, John D. *The Organization and Role of the Army Service Forces, United States Army in World War II.* Washington, D.C.: Office of the Chief of Military History, Department of the Army, 1954.

Moore, John Hammond. *The Faustball Tunnel: German POWs in America and Their Great Escape.* New York: Random House, 1978.

Morrison, Elting E. *Turmoil and Tradition: A Study of the Life and Times of Henry L. Stimson.* Boston: Houghton Mifflin Company, 1960.

Pabel, Reinhold. *Enemies Are Human.* Philadelphia: John C. Winston Company, 1955.

Prange, Gordon. *At Dawn We Slept: The Untold Story of Pearl Harbor.* New York: Penguin Books, 1982.

Shirer, William L. *The Rise and Fall of the Third Reich.* New York: Simon & Schuster, Inc., 1960.

Tonan, Jiri. *Index of the Geneva Convention for the Protection of War Victims.* Institute Henry-Dunant Scientific Collection #2, 194 pp., Leiden.

Weglyn, Michi. *Years of Infamy: The Untold Story of America's Concentration Camps.* Seattle: University of Washington Press, 1996.

Whittingham, Richard. *Martial Justice.* Claremore, OK: Country Lane Press for the Fort Leavenworth Historical Society, 1988.

Periodicals

Baum, Vicki. "Land of the Free." *Collier's*, August 9, 1944.

Collier's. "On Pampering Prisoners." August 12, 1944.

Hartt, John. "Arizona's Tombstone Days Echoed as POWs Flashed Towel Swastika." *Atlanta Constitution*, April 10, 1945.

———. "Desert Town Protests 'Coddling' Nazi Prisoners." *Atlanta Constitution*, March 12, 1945.

Newsweek. "Anger at Nazi Atrocities Is Rising but United States Treats Prisoners Fairly." May 7, 1945, 58.

———. "Swastika Over Arizona." February 26, 1945.
Prologue 41, no. 2 (Summer 2009).
Time. "Behind the Wire." June 21, 1943.
———. "Escape in Arizona." January 8, 1945.

Newspapers

Arizona Republic, various
Fort Leavenworth News, 1945
Fort Leavenworth Reception Center News, 1952
Kansas City Star, July 10, July 14, August 25, 1945
Phoenix Gazette, various

INDEX

R

S

T

U

V

W

Y

Z

ABOUT THE AUTHOR

Jane Eppinga has a BA and BS from the University of Arizona in Tucson. She has more than three hundred articles and short stories to her credit. Her biography of Henry Ossian Flipper, West Point's first black graduate, was part of a package presented to President W.J. Clinton as a successful appeal to have Flipper posthumously pardoned. Her previous Arcadia Publishing books include *Tucson, Arizona*; *Nogales, Arizona, Life and Times on the Frontier*; and *Tombstone: Apache Junction and the Superstition Mountains*. She has also published *They Made Their Mark: An Illustrated History of the Society of Woman Geographers* with Globe Pequot. On July 5, 2009, she presented a paper based on the latter book before the Tenth International Interdisciplinary Congress in Madrid, Spain. Her book about southern Arizona cemeteries was released in March 2014. She presented a paper to the Pearl S. Buck Symposium in China in September 2015.